Assessing and Treating Culturally Diverse Clients

MULTICULTURAL ASPECTS OF COUNSELING SERIES

SERIES EDITOR
Paul Pedersen, Ph.D., *Syracuse University*

EDITORIAL BOARD

Volumes in This Series

1. **Increasing Multicultural Understanding: A Comprehensive Model**
   by Don C. Locke

2. **Preventing Prejudice: A Guide for Counselors and Educators**
   by Joseph G. Ponterotto and Paul B. Pedersen

3. **Improving Intercultural Interactions: Modules for Cross-Cultural Training Programs**
   edited by Richard W. Brislin and Tomoko Yoshida

4. **Assessing and Treating Culturally Diverse Clients: A Practical Guide**
   by Freddy A. Paniagua

5. **Overcoming Unintentional Racism in Counseling and Therapy: A Practitioner's Guide to Intentional Intervention**
   by Charles R. Ridley

6. **Multicultural Counseling With Teenage Fathers: A Practical Guide**
   by Mark S. Kiselica

Assessing and Treating Culturally Diverse Clients

A Practical Guide

Freddy A. Paniagua

Multicultural Aspects of Counseling Series 4

Multicultural Aspects of Counseling Series 4

SAGE Publications
International Educational and Professional Publisher
Thousand Oaks   London   New Delhi

For information address:

SAGE Publications, Inc.
2455 Teller Road
Thousand Oaks, California 91320
E-mail: order@sagepub.com

SAGE Publications Ltd.
6 Bonhill Street
London EC2A 4PU
United Kingdom

SAGE Publications India Pvt. Ltd.
M-32 Market
Greater Kailash I
New Delhi 110 048 India

Printed in the United States of America

Library of Congress Cataloging-in-Publication Data

Paniagua, Freddy A.
    Assessing and treating culturally diverse clients: a practical
guide / Freddy A. Paniagua
        p. cm. — (Multicultural aspects of counseling series; 4)
    Includes bibliographical references and index.
    ISBN 0-8039-5495-6 (cl). — ISBN 0-8039-5496-4 (pb)
    1. Cross-cultural counseling—United States.   I. Title.
II. Series: Multicultural aspects of counseling series; v. 4
BF637.C6P264   1994
361.3′23′089—dc20   94-17662

        96 97 98 99 10 9 8 7 6 5 4

Sage Production Editor: Diane S. Foster

Contents

Series Editor's Introduction   vii

Preface   xi

Acknowledgments   xv

1. Minority, Multicultural, Race, and Ethnicity Concepts   1

2. General Guidelines for the Assessment and Treatment of Multicultural Groups   5

3. Guidelines for the Assessment and Treatment of African Americans   19

4. Guidelines for the Assessment and Treatment of Hispanics   37

5. Guidelines for the Assessment and Treatment of Asians   55

6. Guidelines for the Assessment and Treatment of American Indians   73

7. Guidelines for the Prevention of Attrition With African American, American Indian, Asian, and Hispanic Clients   91

8. Guidelines for Evaluating and Using the Epidemiological
   Mental Health Literature With Multicultural Groups   95

9. Using Culturally Biased Instruments   105

   References   125

   Index   135

   About the Author   141

Series Editor's Introduction

Of all the practical issues of counseling being addressed by the **Multicultural Aspects of Counseling** series, none is more urgent than accurate assessment. *Assessing and Treating Culturally Diverse Clients* does an excellent job both in helping counselors be more accurate in their assessments and in being able to compensate for cultural biases in assessment measures through skilled interpretation. Now that the literature on counseling is quite clear about cultural bias in the practice of counseling, some more extremist responses are for disregarding any measure proven to be culturally biased. Paniagua guides the counselor in working with and using less-than-perfect measures and compensating for any cultural bias through a skilled interpretation of data from those measures. As research on counseling becomes more accurate in identifying cultural bias in counseling measures, we will need to know how we can continue to use those measures meaningfully without either discarding them or imposing their biases on culturally different clients.

Assessing and Treating Culturally Diverse Clients is divided into nine chapters defining the concepts and general guidelines for assessment in multicultural populations and providing specific guidelines for populations of African Americans, Hispanics, Asians, and American Indians. The last three chapters deal with issues of prevention, epidemiology, and guidelines for accurately interpreting data from culturally biased measures. Each chapter specifies practical guidelines that can be immediately useful to counselors.

Research literature suggests that a skilled counselor has completed more than one-half her or his diagnosis of a client's problem by the time a client has come into the room, been greeted, responded to the greeting, and is seated. This broad definition helps the counselor "assess" the interview, modify counseling approaches appropriately for each culturally different client, assess a client's strength or weakness, measure the complex and dynamic changes in culturally different clients during counseling, and measure the impact both of what is said and what is not said in the interview. To be less adequate in assessing the client's cultural context is not only unethical, it is ineffective.

The current generation of practicing counselors was trained in academic programs where cultural differences were much less frequently emphasized than they are today. As a result of this deficiency, many counselors may be continuing to suffer from cultural encapsulation and the self-reference criterion in their counseling practice. *Assessing and Treating Culturally Diverse Clients* is an attempt to help those counselors to be more accurate in their assessment and more appropriate in their treatment of culturally different clients in a user-friendly and helpful strategy for professional development.

For those counselors now in preservice training courses, this book guarantees that the hard questions about multicultural assessment will be addressed in the classroom, along with the more traditional literature in support of accurate measurement. In addition to the practical guidelines offered by this book, the reader is introduced to a rich resource of published literature that elaborates in more depth on each specific topical aspect of multicultural assessment. The field of counseling is rapidly changing in response to increased awareness of cultural similarities and differences. This book is designed to help the counselor keep up with those changes.

The **Multicultural Aspects of Counseling** series defines culture broadly rather than narrowly. That means that, in addition to ethnographic variables (nationality, ethnicity, language, religion), the series also focuses on demographic variables (such as age, gender, place of residence), status variables (such as social, economic, educational), and affiliation variables (formal as well as informal). This inclusive definition of culture allows each of these social system variables to become salient, according to the demands of each sociocultural context.

The **Multicultural Aspects of Counseling** series takes a psychological perspective, but that perspective is applied to disciplines outside of psychology as well. Multicultural assessment requires an interdisciplinary focus because the problems themselves are dynamic as different aspects of the problems become evident. For this reason, the **Multicultural Aspects of Counseling** series is defined broadly enough to include a great variety of assessments and measures. Volumes in the series emphasize the educational model rather more than the medical model in approach to counseling. The client is viewed as a student or trainee rather than as a patient. The client may be healthy and normal, but may have serious problems where some form of counseling is appropriate.

Assessing and Treating Culturally Diverse Clients will increase the reader's awareness through challenging culturally biased assumptions, the reader's knowledge through presenting factual information about assessment methods and measures, the reader's skill through identifying right actions based on appropriate awareness and accurate knowledge. This volume will stimulate the reader to consider a variety of different approaches to assessment according to a client's culture differences. It is intended to stimulate readers to reavaluate their own approach to assessment of themselves, their client's, and their approach to counseling.

Paul Pedersen

Syracuse University

Preface

WHY THIS BOOK WAS WRITTEN

Four major multicultural groups in mental health practices are African Americans, American Indians, Asians, and Hispanics. A major task for practitioners across all mental health disciplines (psychology, psychiatry, social work, family therapy, and the like) is to learn and apply skills that indicate that they are culturally competent in the assessment and treatment of clients from these groups. Relevant questions in the assessment and treatment of multicultural groups include:

- What should a practitioner do during the first meeting or session with an African American client versus an Asian client?
- Would a practitioner treat an American Indian client with the same therapeutic approach as a Hispanic client?
- What exactly would a practitioner do to assess or treat these groups differently?
- What are some examples of cross-cultural skills a practitioner should display to minimize biases when assessing clients from different multicultural groups?

These questions are not only clinically relevant, but the failure to answer them and to demonstrate their use in clinical practices may be considered an example of lacking cultural competence and a violation of ethical principles. For example, in the code of ethics from the American Psychological Association (1992), mental health professionals "must be aware of cultural, individual, and role differences, including those due to age, gender, *race, ethnicity, national origin, religion . . . language,* and *socioeconomic status*" (pp. 3-4, italics added). A violation of this principle would be considered a case of "unfair discriminatory practices" (American Psychological Association, 1992, p. 3). In addition, the written and oral exams required for licensure in the practice of psychology, psychiatry, social work, and other mental health professions include items dealing with the understanding and application of cultural variables that might impact the assessment and treatment of multicultural groups seeking mental health services.

Excellent literature is available to help mental health practitioners in the development and application of cross-cultural skills in their clinical contacts with multicultural groups (Bamford, 1991; Berry, Poortinga, Segall, & Darsen, 1992; Comas-Díaz & Griffith, 1988; Dana, 1993a; Gaw, 1993a; Ho, 1992; Koslow & Salett, 1989; Lefley & Pedersen, 1987; McAdoo, 1993; Pedersen, 1986; Seijo, Gomez, & Freidenberg, 1991; Sue & Sue, 1990; Tharp, 1991). However, practical guidelines in the assessment and treatment of these groups is either dispersed across the literature (Comas-Díaz, 1988; Dana, 1993a; Koslow & Salett, 1989) or mixed with discussions of philosophical, political, and theoretical issues regarding the assessment and treatment of such groups (Berry et al., 1992; Sue & Sue, 1990). Practitioners interested in self-training regarding cultural competence in the assessment and treatment of multicultural groups lack an integrative approach in which such guidelines are summarized in a single text.

In addition, discussion of multicultural issues in mental health (particularly in the areas of treatment and assessment) is evolving rapidly; practitioners may be having a difficult time keeping up with this movement while engaging in their routine clinical practices. The main goal of *Assessing and Treating Culturally Diverse Clients* is to provide an integrative and practical answer to the following question: What exactly should a mental health practitioner do or not do to demonstrate cultural competence and avoid unfair discriminatory practices during the assessment and treatment of African American, American Indian, Asian, and Hispanic clients?

Overview

It is important to emphasize that descriptions of cultural variables in this book reflect generalizations that may not be true for all members of a group or for each subgroup in a given group (e.g., in the case of Hispanics, the subgroup of Cubans versus the subgroup of Mexican Americans). As noted by Sue and Sue (1990), it is erroneous to believe that all African Americans are the same, that all Hispanics are the same, that all Asians are the same, or that all American Indians are the same. Differences across these groups and subgroups exist in terms of primary language (particularly among Asians), generational status (e.g., early versus later immigrants), acculturation, and socioeconomic status (Sue & Sue, 1987, 1990). However, these groups and subgroups do share some cultural variables often considered as relevant in the assessment and treatment of all multicultural groups, regardless of group identity (e.g., all groups and subgroups prefer family relationships, emphasizing the extended family rather than the nuclear family). This sharing of cultural variables might be termed "cultural commonalities" (a term adopted from Chung, 1992).

The main purpose of *Assessing and Treating Culturally Diverse Clients* is to provide a summary of examples of cultural commonalities across groups (Chapters 2, 7, 8, and 9) and within subgroups (Chapters 3, 4, 5, and 6) that clinicians can use to guide their clinical practices with African America, Hispanic, Asian, and American Indian clients.

The book encompasses nine chapters. Chapter 1 proposes a tentative explanation for the growing use of the terms "multicultural" or "diversity," and less emphasis on the term "minority" in the literature. This chapter also includes a brief discussion on the distinction between the terms "race" and "ethnicity."

Chapter 2 presents an overview of general guidelines regarding the development of a therapeutic relationship that seems relevant to the four culturally diverse groups included in this text. In Chapters 3 through 6, in addition to an overview of demographic characteristics, practical guidelines are described for African American (Chapter 3), Hispanic (Chapter 4), Asian (Chapter 5), and American Indian clients (Chapter 6): guidelines on cultural variables that may affect assessment and treatment, guidelines for the first session, and guidelines for conducting psychotherapy. Chapter 7 presents a summary of practical guidelines for understanding and preventing attrition among the target multicultural groups. Chapter 8 is an attempt to assist practitioners in the critical review and evaluation of epidemiological studies dealing with the prevalence and incidence of mental disorders among the four multicultural groups.

Chapter 9 makes an obvious point: Most measures or assessments used by practitioners today with African American, American Indian, Asian, and Hispanic clients are culturally biased. However, because of practical and economical reasons, it may not be advisable to recommend that practitioners should not use these measures and assessments. A better alternative would be to train practitioners to use culturally biased measures. Practitioners need to know how to recognize such biases and how to accommodate data accurately and appropriately to be meaningful and helpful with culturally diverse clients.

Acknowledgments

I am indebted to many people whose support and advice played a major role in the preparation of this book. I want to thank F. M. Baker (University of Maryland) and Sharon Nelson-Le Gall (University of Pittsburgh) for their review of Chapter 3 (African Americans) and valuable suggestions. Richard H. Dana (Portland State University) reviewed the guidelines involving the use of the epidemiology of mental health literature with multicultural groups (Chapter 8) and the guidelines concerning the use of culturally biased instruments (Chapter 9). He sent me an extensive commentary regarding ways to improve these chapters, and I am grateful to him for his comments. Derald W. Sue (California State University at Hayward) and Anh Nga Nguyen (University of Oklahoma Health Sciences Center) assisted me with Chapter 5 (Asians), and I also want to thank them for their comments. D. W. Sue also reviewed Chapter 2 (general guidelines); I particularly thank him for updating the references on Asian Americans. I thank Stanley Sue (University of California, Los Angeles) for reviewing portions of Chapters 1 and 2, particularly in relation to the discussion on cultural mismatch and racial mismatch.

Arthur McDonald (Dull Knife Memorial College) reviewed the chapter on American Indian clients, and I wish to thank him for making me aware of several sensitive issues in the assessment and treatment of this group. Lillian Comas-Díaz made substantial revisions regarding guidelines in the

assessment and treatment of Hispanic clients (Chapter 4), including trans-
lating terms from English into Spanish, providing a better interpretation
of the acknowledgment of spiritual issues by Hispanic clients during the
first session, and enhancing the bibliography dealing with the assessment
and treatment of Hispanic clients. I thank her for her effort and time in
revising these materials.

Sylvia Z. Ramirez (University of Texas at Austin) and Sylvia Linares
were clinical fellows under my supervision at the time I was organizing
my thoughts to write this book. I discussed many of the topics in this text
with them, and I thank them for their suggestions. I also want to thank
Sylvia Ramirez for reviewing Chapters 4 and 8, as well as for her suggestion to include additional cultural variables leading to a better understanding of the assessment and treatment of Hispanic clients.

I have spent many hours over the last 5 years discussing cross-cultural
issues with Israel Cuellar (University of Texas—Pan American University
at Edinburg). He was the first person (as far as I can remember) who
encouraged me to write this book, and he reviewed Chapters 4, 8, and 9. I
deeply thank him for his comments and suggestions on how to improve
these chapters.

I thank Paul Pedersen, Series Editor, who was instrumental in the final
preparation of this book for publication. He spent many hours reading each
chapter and making sure that the book reflects practical guidelines for
clinicians interested in the assessment and treatment of multicultural
groups and that the book contains minimal rhetoric about multiculturalism.

I also want to thank the staff at Sage Publications for their time and effort
in the preparation of the book. I particularly thank Marquita Flemming,
Diane Foster, Dale Mary Grenfell, and Deirdre McDonald Greene for their
assistance and technical advice.

I want especially to thank my spouse, Sandra A. Black (Sam), and my
son, Robert Alexander Paniagua (Rap), for their support and patience
throughout the completion of this book.

Finally, it is important to recognize that this topic is extremely sensitive
and that I am responsible for any error or misunderstanding the reader may
find in the text. I would appreciate comments or suggestions from readers
for consideration in future editions of this book. Please send your comments to Sage Publications, 2455 Teller Road, Thousand Oaks, CA 91320.

1

Minority, Multicultural, Race, and Ethnicity Concepts

Minority Groups Versus
Multicultural Groups

In general, the term "minority" represents both a number and certain disadvantages in terms of socioeconomic status (Ho, 1992, 1993; Sue & Sue, 1990; Wilkinson, 1993). In the United States, Anglo Americans or whites are not considered a "minority group" because there are too many of them (approximately 207,754 million in 1991) and their socioeconomic status is often higher than other groups in the United States (U.S. Bureau of the Census, 1992). On the other hand, African Americans are considered a minority group because they number approximately 30.8 million (U.S. Bureau of the Census, 1992) and their socioeconomic status is lower than that of the "majority" (i.e., whites). Other examples of minority groups in terms of number and socioeconomic status in 1991 were American Indians, Asians/Pacific Islanders, and Hispanics (U.S. Bureau of the Census, 1992). However, the term minority may not be appropriate for three reasons: discrepancy in income levels across minority groups; the impact of minority groups on other groups; and the implication that the term minority is another term for "inferiority" in the mind of some members of such groups.

Discrepancy in Income Levels
Across Minority Groups

When comparing median income levels across minority groups (e.g., Asians versus African Americans), one finds a discrepancy in income levels across the groups. For example, in 1991 the median income for the Asian and Pacific Islander population (e.g., Japanese, Chinese, Filipino, Hawaiian) was $42,245 and the median income for African Americans was $21,423; the national U.S. median income was $35,262 (U.S. Bureau of the Census, 1992). Asians, Pacific Islanders, and African Americans are examples of minority groups in this country in terms of their numbers in comparison with Anglo Americans. In 1991, however, the Asian and Pacific Islander population reported a median income far above the national average.

A similar point can be made by comparing income levels across subgroups within the same ethnic group. For example, the median income for Cubans (a subgroup of Hispanics) in 1991 was $31,439, whereas the median income for Puerto Ricans (another subgroup of Hispanics) was $18,008. In addition, in 1991 37.5% of Puerto Rican families and 40.6% of Puerto Rican persons were below the poverty level, in comparison with only 13.8% (families) and 16.9% (persons) reported by Cubans (U.S. Bureau of the Census, 1992). Cubans and Puerto Ricans are examples of minority groups in the United States, but Cubans have a better standard of living in the United States than Puerto Ricans.

Therefore, although a person could be considered as a minority because that person is a member of a small number of people in comparison with the majority, that person may not share the same minority status when income level is considered (either between minority groups or between subgroups within the same group).

Impact of Minority Groups
Upon Other Groups

Another problem with the use of the term minority is that it does not take into consideration the impact of the size of a minority group upon another minority group (Wilkinson, 1986). For example, many African Americans and Hispanics reside in Florida. However, in several sections of Florida (e.g., Miami), African Americans constitute a minority group, whereas Hispanics constitute a majority group. Both groups are examples of minority populations when the number of people in the United States is considered in the definition of minority. In such sections of Florida, however, Hispanics constitute the majority. A similar comparison could be made in the case of the population of the Lower Rio Grande Valley of Texas (which is concentrated around the U.S.-Mexican border). In this region, Mexican Americans are the majority; other Hispanics (e.g., Puerto Ricans, Cubans), Asians, African Americans, and American Indians are minority groups.

The Concept of Minority as a
Case for Inferiority

Practitioners should be aware that some people do not want to be called "minority" because this term implies inferiority and a sense of superiority by those in the majority (i.e., Anglo Americans). For example, in a letter sent to the *San Antonio Express News,* a Hispanic wrote, "when an individual labels me a 'minority,' I feel small, weak and irrelevant. On the other hand, 'ethnically diverse American' is empowering and more accurate" (R. E. Martinez, 1993, p. 5B). Furthermore, McAdoo (1993) points out that a major reason to avoid the term minority is that "it has an insidious implication of inferiority. . . . A sense of superiority is assumed by those of the implied superior status" (p. 6).

Thus it seems that the term minority may not be applicable when issues involving income level, the impact of minority groups upon other minority groups, and the potential use of the term as synonymous with inferiority are considered (Kim, McLeod, & Shantzis, 1992; McAdoo, 1993; Wilkinson, 1986). More appropriate terms include "multicultural" or "diversity" populations/groups. These terms emphasize the fact that groups may be among the few in terms of their number in the United States, but differ in terms of cultural values. This concept (instead of the concept of minority group) is gradually appearing in the literature (Dana, 1993a).

In the assessment and treatment of people with mental disorders, a practical guideline is to emphasize the ways different multicultural groups express their cultural values, their views about the world, and their place in this society, rather than an emphasis upon the minority group per se. For example, African Americans and Anglo Americans are examples of multicultural groups in the United States. Other multicultural groups seen with less frequency in mental health services in the United States include Greeks, Italians, Irish, Polish Americans, and West Indian Islanders (Allen, 1988; Jalali, 1988). *Assessing and Treating Culturally Diverse Groups* summarizes practical guidelines in the assessment and treatment of four multicultural groups often seen in mental health services: African Americans, American Indians, Asians, and Hispanics.

Race Versus Ethnicity

A controversy exists regarding the interchangeable use of the terms "race" and "ethnicity." Both terms seem to label two different processes (Berry, Pooringan, Segall, & Darsen, 1992; Betancourt & López, 1993; Wilkinson, 1993). An understanding of these processes is an important factor in the assessment and treatment of multicultural groups. As noted by Wilkinson (1993), race "is a category of persons who are related by a common heredity or ancestry and who are perceived and responded to in terms of external features or traits" (p. 19). Ethnicity, on the other hand, often refers to "a shared culture and lifestyles" (Wilkinson, 1993, p. 19). An individual could belong to a particular race without sharing ethnic identity with that race. For example, the fact that two Hispanic clients share a common heredity or ancestry does not necessarily mean that they also share the same ethnic identity (e.g., culture, values, lifestyles, beliefs, norms). This difference in ethnic identity may be explained in terms of the process of acculturation (see Chapter 2), which may have a tremendous implication in the assessment and treatment of many diverse groups. Thus an important guideline in treating multicultural mental health patients is not to assume that because two clients share the same racial group they also share the same ethnicity (e.g., values and lifestyles).

2

General Guidelines for the Assessment and Treatment of Multicultural Groups

This chapter summarizes general guidelines, recommended in the literature (Dana, 1993a; Ho, 1992, 1993), for assessing and treating the four multicultural groups discussed in this book.

The Development of a Therapeutic Relationship

A therapeutic relationship seems paramount with all multicultural groups (Ho, 1992; Sue & Sue, 1990). In general, the development of such a relationship involves three levels.

The *conceptual* level includes the client's and the therapist's perception of sincerity, openness, honesty, motivation, empathy, sensitivity, inquiring concerns, and credibility. The *behavioral* level includes the client's perception of the therapist as competent in his or her profession, which may encompass issues regarding the training of the therapist as well as evidence in the specialization in the assessment and treatment of particular mental health problems (e.g., depression). The behavioral level also reflects the therapist's perception of his or her client as competent in terms of the client's ability to follow direction and to use skills to self-implement the treatment plan as discussed between the therapist and the client.

The *cultural* level generally includes two hypotheses (Paniagua, Wassef, O'Boyle, Linares, & Cuellas, 1993; Tharp, 1991). The *cultural compatibility hypothesis* suggests that the assessment and treatment of multicultural groups are enhanced if racial and ethnic barriers between the client and the therapist are minimized. As these racial and ethnic differences approach zero, the therapist is effective in terms of providing culturally sensitive assessment and treatment to a particular group (Dana, 1993a; López, López, & Fong, 1991; Sue & Sue, 1990). For example, this hypothesis suggests that the assessment and treatment of an African American client is enhanced if the therapist is also African American. The racial/ethnic similarity in turn reinforces the client-therapist therapeutic relationship.

However, the cultural compatibility hypothesis may not be practical in clinical practices for several reasons. In a test of this hypothesis, Sue, Fujino, Hu, Takeuchi, and Zane (1991) found that racial "match failed to be a significant predictor of treatment outcome, except for Mexican Americans" (p. 539). The other groups in this study were Asian Americans, African Americans, and whites. These authors also found that racial match "appears to have a much greater impact on length of treatment [defined as dropping out and number of sessions] than on outcome" (p. 539).

Many members of culturally diverse groups (particularly African Americans) have been part of outcome research conducted by white investigators; the overall conclusion is that the race or ethnicity of the investigator has no effect on outcome (Sue, 1988). This point is particularly evident in the case of behavioral approaches (including behavior analysis, behavior therapy, and cognitive-behavioral modification; Paniagua & Baer, 1981), which are currently dominated by white investigators and clinicians. Many research subjects included in these approaches have been selected from a wide range of culturally diverse groups; the results clearly show the effectiveness of such approaches in the treatment of clients from any race or ethnic background (Kolko, 1987). In fact, it is widely believed by culturally diverse clinicians and investigators that behavioral approaches are probably the most effective strategies in the assessment and treatment of the four multicultural groups discussed here (Boyd-Franklin, 1989; Walker & LaDue, 1985; Yamamoto, Silva, Justice, Chang, & Leong, 1993). This is because these strategies are authoritative, concrete, action oriented, and emphasize an immediate, focused learning—factors generally preferred by these groups (Boyd-Franklin, 1989; Walker & LaDue, 1985).

Sue (1988) advises that racial match may lead to cultural mismatch, but that racial "mismatches do not necessarily imply cultural mismatches, because therapists and clients from different [racial] groups may share similar values, lifestyles, and experiences" (p. 306). That is, in terms of the distinction between race and ethnicity discussed in Chapter 1, the therapist and the client may share the same racial group (e.g., both are Hispanic) but they may not share the same ethnicity (e.g., they have different values and lifestyles). For example, highly acculturated Hispanic therapists working with less acculturated Hispanic clients may result in cultural mismatches (e.g., the therapist and the client do not share similar lifestyles and values), regardless of the fact that both therapist and client share the same racial group. Similarly, white therapists working with highly acculturated Hispanic clients may result in cultural matches (e.g., both share Western culture, values, and traditions), regardless of the racial mismatch.

Because of a history of hostile relations among some Asian nations (e.g., wars between Chinese and Japanese, Japanese and Koreans, Chinese and Vietnamese), it may be not practical to recommend the applicability of the cultural compatibility hypothesis with these groups (Yamamoto et al., 1993). If an older Japanese client is assigned for assessment and evaluation to a Chinese therapist, this relationship may create tension and mistrust, leading to potential failures in the treatment of that client. Thus, before an Asian therapist is recommended in the assessment and treatment of Asian clients, it may be appropriate to explore the potential impact of historical events.

Because of the problems with the cultural compatibility hypothesis, a second hypothesis has been proposed. This alternative hypothesis is known as the *universalistic argument* (Dana, 1993a; Tharp, 1991). In this argument, effective assessment and treatment are the same across all multicultural groups independently of the issue of client-therapist racial/ethnic differences or similarities. This hypothesis probably explains the current emphasis on the training of Anglo American therapists in the assessment and treatment of the four major multicultural groups discussed in this book. The hypothesis proposes that what is relevant in the assessment and treatment of multicultural groups is evidence that the therapist can display both cultural sensitivity (i.e., awareness of cultural variables that may affect assessment and treatment) and cultural competence (i.e., translation of this awareness into behavior leading to effective assessment and treatment of the particular multicultural group; see Atkinson & Wampold, 1993, p. 247; Baker, 1988, p. 157) . Thus, in terms of this hypothesis, white therapists are as effective as African American therapists in the assessment and treatment of African American clients as long as these two qualities (sensitivity and competence) are manifested in the clinical practice of the therapists. The hypothesis also suggests that the fact that a therapist and his or her client share the same race and ethnicity (e.g., Hispanic therapist and client sharing similar values and lifestyles) does not guarantee the effectiveness of assessment and treatment of the client; this therapist must also show evidence of sensitivity and competency to enhance the effectiveness of assessment and treatment strategies, regardless of the shared race/ethnicity dimension in the therapist-client relationship.

Two additional issues in the universalistic hypothesis include the concepts of credibility and giving (Sue & Sue, 1990; Sue & Zane, 1987). *Credibility* is the client's perception that the therapist is effective and trustworthy; *giving* deals with the client's recognition that the therapist has provided something of value in the client-therapist relationship. In summary, the null hypothesis states that the ability to communicate credibly and in a giving, cultural sensitive manner and to exhibit cultural competency during the assessment and treatment of multicultural groups is more important than any similarity in the therapist's and client's racial membership (Baker, 1988; Tharp, 1991).

Materials presented here discuss how practitioners from any racial group (including Anglos) can enhance or develop cultural sensitivity and competency in the assessment and treatment of African American, American Indian, Asian, and Hispanic clients, regardless of racial/ethnic differences or similarities between practitioners and their clients.

Acculturation

Acculturation is a variable that must be considered during the assessment and treatment of the four multicultural groups discussed in this book (Dana, 1993a; Ho, 1992). In general, acculturation may be defined in terms of the degree of integration of new cultural patterns into the original cultural patterns (Dana, 1993a; Moyerman & Forman, 1992). The process of acculturation can be internal and external.

In the internal process of acculturation, changes in cultural patterns may occur when a diverse group moves from one U.S. region to another U.S. region (e.g., from one city to another within the same state or across states). For example, when American Indians living in Arizona, New Mexico, or other states with a large number of reservations move from their reservations to cities, they experience the impact of a societal lifestyle quite different from the lifestyle they experienced on the reservations. Competition and individualism are two values with little relevance to American Indians who reside on reservations. These values, however, are extremely important for anyone who resides outside a reservation. In this example, the group simply moves from one area to another within the United States; and the assimilation of new values and lifestyles in the new area is a function of the process of internal acculturation. The impact of the internal process of acculturation would be minimal if an American Indian were to move from one reservation to another reservation in the United States.

The internal process of acculturation is further illustrated by Hispanics residing in certain areas of New York City who move to certain areas in Florida (e.g., Miami). The impact of acculturation as an internal process would be minimal in comparison with a move from New York City to another city, such as Lawrence, Kansas, with few shared cultural patterns between Hispanics and residents. Another example is Mexican Americans who reside on the U.S-Mexican border (particularly in the Lower Rio Grande Valley of Texas, including Edinburg, Brownsville, McCallen, and Harlingen). Mexican Americans who move from this region of the United States to another region resembling little of Mexican American cultural patterns (e.g., Washington, DC) would experience a difficult internal acculturation process. Mexican Americans who move from the U.S.-Mexican border into San Antonio, Texas, though, would not experience that internal process of acculturation (or its impact would be minimal) because many Mexican Americans residing on the U.S.-Mexican border and Mexican Americans residing in San Antonio share similar cultural patterns.

In the external process of acculturation, a person moves from his or her country of origin into another country. This process is experienced by Hispanics and Asians who move to the United States. The effects of the external acculturation process are less dramatic when immigrants move to the United States and reside in cities that resemble the norms, cultural patterns, and values of their home cities. This is the case of most Hispanics from Cuba, the Dominican Republic, and Puerto Rico residing in New York City and Miami, as well as Mexicans who move to U.S. cities located on the U.S.-Mexican border. Hispanics residing in such U.S. cities not only encounter people who can understand their language, but also find people from their countries of origin who share many of their cultural values (e.g., folk beliefs, customs, music). The effect of the external acculturation process is more dramatic when a person moves to the United States and resides in a city with little similarity to that person's original cultural patterns.

Levels of Acculturation

It is also important to determine the potential impact of different levels of acculturation upon the assessment and treatment of a client. These levels can be defined in terms of number of years in the internal or external acculturation process, age at which the client entered such process, and country of origin. The general assumption is that younger clients are more easily acculturated than older clients, and that as the number of years in this process increases, the level of acculturation also increases. In terms of the country of origin, the main assumption is that a racial group tends to show a higher level of acculturation depending on their country of origin. For example, a client from the Dominican Republic residing in New York City is more easily acculturated than a client from Vietnam residing in the same city, because the Dominican experienced (in his or her country of origin) a great deal of U.S. cultural values prior to entering the United States including dressing style, music, language (many Dominicans speak English prior to entering the United States), and a competitive approach.

Chapter 8 (Table 8.1) includes examples of acculturation scales recommended for multicultural groups described in this book. If the therapist does not have not enough time to conduct a thorough screening of acculturation using the scales in Chapter 8, Figure 2.1 provides a brief scale for the assessment of three significant variables in the process of acculturation: generation, language preferred, and social activity (Burnam, Hough, Karnp, Escobar, & Telles, 1987; Cuellar, Harris, & Jasso, 1980; Suinn, Rickard-Figueroa, Lew, & Vigil, 1987). For example, family members in the fifth generation are considered highly acculturated in comparison with members in the first generation. In terms of language preferred, the client should be asked a general question covering most situations in which a certain language is preferred (e.g., with children, with parents, with co-workers). In the case of social activity, a similar approach is recommended. For example, a Mexican American client may be asked "When you listen to music and go to a restaurant to eat, would you do these things with Mexican Americans only, with Mexican Americans mostly, with Mexican Americans and other racial groups mostly (e.g., African Americans, whites, Asians, American Indians), with a different racial group mostly (e.g., whites), or only with a different racial group?"

The following acculturation scores (suggested by Burnam et al., 1987) are recommended for the abbreviated acculturation scale.

1 to 1.75 = low acculturation
1.76 to 3.25 = medium acculturation
3.26 to 5 = high acculturation

To obtain these scores, add all values checked across variables and divide them by the total number of items checked. For example, if the client checked 1 for the first item across each variable, the total score would be

Instructions: Please check only one item from the group of generation items, language preferred items, and social activity items.

My generation is:

First	Second	Third	Fourth	Fifth
(1)	(2)	(3)	(4)	(5)

The language I prefer to use is:

Mine Only	Mostly Mine	Both Mine and English	Mostly English	Only English
(1)	(2)	(3)	(4)	(5)

I prefer to engage in social activities with:

Only Within Racial Group	Mostly Within Racial Group	Within/Between Racial Groups	Mostly With a Different Racial Group	Only With a Different Racial Group
(1)	(2)	(3)	(4)	(5)

Total Score:
Number of Items Checked:
Acculturation Score (Total Score/Number of Items Checked):

The level of acculturation for this client is (circle one):
Low   Medium   High

Figure 2.1. Brief Acculturation Scale

1 (3/3, or low acculturation score). If the client checked 2, 2, and 3 for the generational, language, and social activity variables, the overall acculturation score would be 2.3 (medium acculturation score).

Use of Translators

The use of translators is often necessary with clients who have limited English proficiency. This is particularly true in the assessment and treatment of Asian, Mexican American, and Hispanic clients. However, Martinez (1986) recommends that clinicians should avoid the use of translators for two main reasons. First, the translator introduces a third person into the psychotherapy process, which could lead to distortion and misinterpretation of the client's verbalizations. Omissions, additions, and substitutions are examples of common distortions or errors associated with translation in the practice of psychotherapy (Bamford, 1991). Second, clients may find the presence of the translator disagreeable. In addition, the translator may be unable to express the original speaker's thoughts, which could lead to confusing and misleading information; more severe psychiatric diagnoses may be used when the client is not interviewed in his or her own language; dropout rates may increase because of the client's inability to understand English; and noncompliance behavior may increase (Seijo, Gomez, & Freidenberg, 1991). However, the use of translators may be an unavoidable issue for many clinicians.

If translators are used, the following guidelines are recommended (Bamford, 1991; Gaw, 1993b; Ho, 1982; Westermeyer, 1993).

1. Clinicians should try to use translators who share the client's racial/ethnic background (e.g., Mexican American clients with Mexican American translators, Cuban clients with Cuban translators) and who have an understanding of the variability in linguistic expressions (e.g., *mal puesto* among Mexican Americans and *brujeria* among Cubans).

2. Clinicians should use translators with training in mental health problems and culture-related syndromes (Chapter 9 provides examples of these syndromes).

3. Clinicians should use a sequential mode of translation (i.e., the client speaks, the translator translates into English, the therapist speaks, the translator translates again).

4. Clinicians should avoid concurrent translation (to prevent fatigue).

5. Clinicians should introduce the translator to the client and ensure that the translator spends time alone with the client talking about events common to them both (e.g., their country of origin, music) to provide the message that the translator can understand the client and facilitate the therapeutic alliance between the client and the therapist.

6. Clinicians should emphasize a sentence-by-sentence translation to avoid forgetting details.

7. Clinicians should avoid technical terms (e.g., "You probably have dysthymia") and should ask the client to describe in her or his own words the problem (e.g., "Tell me what exactly has happened in the last 2 years when you say that you have been feeling very sad").

8. A clinical interview with translation will take twice as long. Thus clinicians must plan ahead for the extra time needed for the translation. If the interview is terminated abruptly, the client may infer that the therapist is not interested in the case.

9. Clinicians should consider the potential effect of the translator on the interpretation of clinical data (i.e., the translator may function as a

mediating variable, affecting the report of symptoms by the client and the clinical diagnosis made by the clinician).

10. Clinicians should consider the level of acculturation of the translator in relation to the client's level of acculturation. The fact that a translator and a client share the same racial group (including sharing the same language) is extremely helpful. But major discrepancies between the translator's level of acculturation and the client's level of acculturation could create problems. For example, acculturated Hispanic translators who believe in the American way of dating may not appreciate the conflicts experienced by Hispanic parents who believe that it is not appropriate for their daughter to go out on a date alone or to engage in sexual relationships without being married.

11. Clinicians should avoid the use of relatives and friends as translators. Relatives and friends are not often objective and could distort the translation process either to minimize or maximize psychopathology, depending upon the context of therapy.

12. Clinicians should avoid the use of bilingual children as translators (particularly when the problem involves the child). The bilingualism of a child could dramatically reverse the hierarchical role of parents who are monolingual or have a limited knowledge of English. This guideline is particularly important in the assessment and treatment of Hispanic and Asian families, in which the authority of parents (especially the father) cannot be reversed.

13. In the case of Asian clients, clinicians should determine the client's dialect before asking for a translator.

Overdiagnosing of Multicultural Groups

The possibility of overdiagnosing clients (i.e., false conclusions regarding pathology or mental problems) from any of the multicultural groups described in this book is an issue clinicians should always keep in mind (Chapter 9 includes further discussion of this issue). "Seeing" pathology or mental health problems in such groups has generally been explained in two ways. First, the psychometric properties of commonly used instruments to screen mental health problems are not generally appropriate in the assessment of problems among diverse groups (Dana, 1993a). Two important problems in the assessment of groups discussed in this text are the use of inappropriate norms for a multicultural group and the lack of cross-cultural validity (i.e., the instrument may not be sensitive to problems in a group different from that used to develop the instrument).

The second explanation is associated with a lack of understanding concerning the impact of cultural variables, norms, and values upon the development of behaviors resembling mental health problems (Dana, 1993a; Ramirez, Wassef, Paniagua, & Linskey, 1993). For example, it is not uncommon among Hispanic clients to report that they have *facultades espirituales* (spiritual faculties), meaning that they can communicate with spirits who live in an invisible world. A client with strong religious beliefs may claim that he or she can communicate with the saints through burning candles or praying. Reports involving "having a conversation with the saints" or "receiving a verbal command from the Virgin Mary" are not uncommon among Hispanics. Spirit possession is also reported by Asian and African American clients. For a clinician unfamiliar with these beliefs, such reports would be seen as examples of severe psychopathology, when, in fact, they are a function of the client's belief system (Bernal & Gutierrez, 1988; Dana, 1993a; Martinez, 1988).

Extended Family

Among African Americans, Hispanics, Asians, and American Indians, the extended family seems to play a major role (Ho, 1982; Sue & Sue, 1990). What is an extended family? The answer should be provided by the client, not by the therapist. An important guideline to remember is not to assume that the client and the therapist share the same definition of an extended family.

For example, it may be a mistake to assume that an aunt is viewed by an African American client as a member of the extended family simply because she is biologically related to the client. As noted by Anderson, Eaddy, and Williams (1990), the client would seek two types of supports before including an aunt in his or her definition of extended family: instrumental supports (e.g., money, clothing, child care) and emotional supports (e.g., counseling and advice). If these supports cannot be provided by the aunt, the client would not include her in his or her interpretation of an extended family.

A guideline for understanding a client's definition of "extension" is the client's description of instrumental and emotional support provided by any member of the community. Persons mentioned by the client with a fundamental role in the provision of such assistance should be considered part of the client's extended family. These persons may include a brother (but not a sister), a priest (but not a grandfather), a friend (but not a uncle), or the manager assigned to the case by welfare agencies (but not the director of these agencies).

The therapist should expect the client to bring to the clinic both biological (e.g., uncles, aunts, sisters) and nonbiological (e.g., friends, minister) members of his or her extended family. In the case of Hispanic clients, nonbiological members often include the *compadre* (cofather) and the *comadre* (comother), who are invited by the client to play an active role in the process of psychotherapy (Comas-Díaz & Griffith, 1988). Among American Indian clients, the elders in the tribe (particularly the head of the tribe) and traditional medicine men and women have a special place in the family; they are seen as an integral part of the extended family (Dana, 1993a; Ho, 1992; Richardson, 1981). In the case of African Americans, church membership is an essential element in the family and it is expected that church members (particularly the minister) would be involved in the solution of family issues (Baker, 1988; Dana, 1993a). In this group, grandparents, sisters, and brothers often play a major role in the extended family (Boyd-Franklin, 1989). Among Asian American and Asian/Pacific Islander clients, the extended family generally does not include individuals (e.g., friends, minister) outside the core family structure (i.e., parents, children, grandparents, and relatives). This is because public admission of problems (including mental health problems) is generally not accepted in these groups (Sue & Sue, 1990). Finally, many Southeast Asian clients (Vietnamese, Cambodians, and Laotians) may place more emphasize on nonbiological persons (e.g., friends) or social agencies (e.g., welfare agencies, community supports) in their definition of extended family than on the nuclear family (e.g., parents). The reason for this is that many refugees either left their family behind in their country of origin or lost family members during war (Mollica & Lavelle, 1988).

Implicit in the above discussion is a distinction between the concepts of extended family tree and family tree. A family tree generally includes a description of the client and his or her immediate relatives. The development of a family tree is generally recommended in the formulation of the genogram (see Ho, 1993, p. 159). In clinical practices, however, the formulation of the family tree may not be a realistic approach when the goal of the genogram is to describe the client's definition of the concept of extended family in terms of biological and nonbiological persons considered essential in the provision of instrumental and emotional supports. The formulation of the genogram in terms of the concept of extended family tree, however, may assist practitioners because it includes both relatives and nonrelatives who provide support to the client. For example, in the case of Hispanic clients, the extended family tree may include the client, children (if any), parents, grandparents, godfather, godmother, a priest, and friends. Similar extended family trees may be formulated with other multicultural groups. Medicine men and women would be included in the extended family tree of American Indian clients. More friends, social agencies, and case managers than relatives would be included in the extended family tree of Southeast Asian clients.

Foster Homes and
the Extended Family

Boyd-Franklin (1989) points out that no inquiry about the extended family can result in placing children in foster homes if the biological parents are not able to take care of them (e.g., because of hospitalization, severe father-mother marital conflicts which may put these children at risk for physical injuries). It is important to ask parents about a member of the extended family (as it is defined by the client) who may be willing to take care of a child (or children) in cases when parents are not able to assume this responsibility. The person selected by the client could be a nonbiological member of the extended family (e.g., a friend, the godfather). If the foster parents (selected from the parents' extended family) and the biological parents do not share the same racial/ethnic background, the therapist should ensure that the foster parents understand the norms, values, beliefs and other cultural aspects of the child's racial/ethnic background and will apply that understanding to real-life situations. For example, in the case of African American children placed with white foster parents, the therapist should recommend special arrangements for the child to participate in activities involving other African American children (e.g., African American church activities; Jackson & Westmoreland, 1992). Similar arrangements are recommended for Hispanic, Asian, and American Indian children placed with foster parents from different racial/ethnic backgrounds. In the case of American Indian children, an additional guideline is strongly recommended: The therapist should not handle foster care issues without an understanding of the Indian Child Welfare Act (discussed in Chapter 6).

Modality of Therapy

In general, African Americans, American Indians, Hispanics, and Asians prefer a therapy process that encompasses a directive approach (i.e., they want to know what the problem is and what to do to solve this problem); an active approach (i.e., what role they will play in the process of psychotherapy); and a structured approach (i.e., what exactly the therapist is recommending to solve the problem; Sue & Sue, 1990). Most forms of psychotherapies are recommended with the four multicultural groups, particularly behavioral approaches (e.g., social-skills training) and family therapy. Chapters 3 through 6 present examples of specific psychotherapies recommended across the four multicultural groups.

The programming of individual psychotherapy (i.e., intervention with only the client) is generally recommended with all groups prior to the scheduling of family therapy (a preferred form of intervention) in those cases when acculturation seems to play a major role in the manifestation of the clinical problem. This is particularly important to remember when the clinical problem involves either marital conflicts (e.g., discrepancies in values, norms, worldview in less acculturated men-more acculturated women relationships) or family problems involving children and adolescents with high levels of acculturation relative to their parents. Jones (1992) points out that some African American adolescents are referred for therapy because "their parents think they are mimicking maladaptive white adolescent behaviors (such as the wearing of punk-style haircuts or interest in heavy metal rock music)" (p. 34). In this example, the assumption is that these African American adolescents may lose their racial/ethnic identity because of the impact of acculturation (i.e., the adoption of the behavior of white adolescents). Jones recommends that individual psychotherapy sessions would be necessary "before initiating productive conjoint family therapy" (p. 34).

How Much Information Is Necessary?

Another general guideline is to avoid collecting a large amount of information. This guideline is particularly important during the first therapeutic contact with the client. The presenting problem should always be emphasized, but without giving the impression that too much information is needed to understand the problem. Most clients in diverse groups (particularly Hispanics) view clinicians who collect a massive amount of information as incompetent in both technical (e.g., little training in collecting significant clinical data) as well as cultural terms (unfamiliarity with the particular group; Seijo et al., 1991). The collection of an extensive amount of information is, of course, an essential strategy in the understanding of the client's problem. This level of information is particularly necessary when formulating the extended family tree. The important guideline to remember in this context is to plan the collection of data gradually across sessions, rather than to give the impression that the therapist wants to know everything in the first 45-minute session. Factors that could facilitate extensive collection of clinical data include the client's belief regarding the therapist's identification of the problem or problems that are considered by the client as essential, the provision of concrete recommendations leading to the solution of such problems through an emphasis upon problem-solving techniques, and the client's perception of credibility. In the absence of such factors, it will be difficult to gather extensive clinical data beyond the preliminary clinical data collected during the first session (e.g., an overview of the problem and perhaps some information about other family members).

The Meaning of "Therapist" Across Multicultural Groups

The therapist must be familiar with the use of the term "therapist" across multicultural groups. Many Asians and African Americans view the therapist as a physician; American Indians view the therapist as a medicine man; and many Hispanics treat the therapist as a folk healer (Comas-Díaz & Griffith, 1988; Ho, 1992; Sue & Sue, 1990).

Understanding the client's definition of therapist could greatly enhance the clinician's ability to manage the problem. For example, American Indian clients do not expect the therapist to recommend synthetic medication for their mental problems; natural herbs are expected. By contrast, many Asian and African American clients expect a discussion of how synthetic medication could control their problems. In the first case, the therapist may be viewed as the medicine man, whereas in the second case the client may perceive the therapist as a physician (Baker, 1988; Richardson, 1981; Sue & Sue, 1990).

3

Guidelines for the Assessment and Treatment of African Americans

In 1991, the African American population was approximately 30.8 million (U.S. Bureau of the Census, 1992). The majority of African Americans lived in the south; smaller numbers lived in the north central, northeastern, and western regions of the United States (U.S. Department of Health & Human Services, 1991). The median income of African Americans in 1991 was $21,423, which was below the national U.S. average of $35,262 and below that of whites ($36,915; U.S. Bureau of the Census, 1992). In 1991, 29.3% of African American families and 31.9% of African American persons were below the poverty line (U.S. Bureau of the Census, 1992), in comparison with 8.1% white families and 10.7% white persons below the poverty level.

Cultural Variables That May
Affect Assessment and Treatment

Racial Labels

Racial labels have been a concern to African Americans for many years (Smith, 1992). Members of this group have been called colored, negro, black, and African American (Smith, 1992). The first three terms emphasize skin color. The last term emphasizes cultural heritage, and it is currently recommended in the literature (Griffith & Baker, 1993; Smith, 1992). The terms colored and negro are considered derogatory and should not be used by practitioners (Smith, 1992). The terms black and African American seem acceptable in a given context. Karkabi (1993) published an interview in the *Houston Chronicle* dealing with the use of both terms; one of the interviewees reported that "if a brother or sister wants to call me black, that's OK. But I would prefer that Anglos call me African American. . . . It acknowledges our ancestry and where we came from, and I think that use of that term by Anglos is more respectful" (p. 5D).

It seems appropriate for a therapist to explore which term (black or African American) is preferred by a client. A practical strategy is to ask the client directly about his or her choice. Some clients prefer to be called black, others prefer the term African American. In both cases, the therapist should honor the wish of the client and stay neutral with respect to current controversies regarding the use of such terms (Smith, 1992, provides an excellent summary of this controversy).

The term African American is used in this book because it is gaining acceptability in the literature (Dana, 1993a; Griffith & Baker, 1993; Ho, 1992; Smith, 1992). Several reasons have been suggested for using the term *African American,* including that it is less stigmatizing (Dana, 1993a), it does not emphasize skin color but includes reference to cultural heritage (Griffith & Baker, 1993), and it formalizes the African connection (Fairchild, 1985).

Familism and Role Flexibility

Both the nuclear family (parents and children) and the extended family (parents, children, relatives, friends, the minister) are important among African Americans (Boyd-Franklin, 1989; Smith, 1981). Because the concept of *familism* among African Americans generally includes both biological (e.g., parents, children, uncles, sisters) and nonbiological (e.g., friends, minister, godfather) members, an important guideline to follow with this group is to formulate a genogram emphasizing the extended family tree (as defined in Chapter 2) rather than simply the biological family tree (a similar guideline is recommended with American Indian, Hispanic, and Asian clients).

Who is the head of the family? Among African American clients the head of the family is not necessarily the father (Baker, 1988). An important issue in these families is *role flexibility*: The mother sometimes plays the role of the father and thus functions as the head of the family. In addition, older children sometimes function as parents or caretakers for younger children. In fact, older African American children may drop out of school to work and help younger children secure a good education (Baker, 1988; Ho, 1992; Smith, 1981). This practice should be carefully considered when a therapist is conducting family therapy involving adolescents; the therapist should not assume that an African American adolescent dropped out of school because of the problem that parents bring to the attention of the therapist.

As noted by Boyd-Franklin (1989), the concept of role flexibility among African American families can be extended to include the parental role assumed by grandfather, grandmother, aunts, and cousins. Therefore an assessment of an African American client should include the identification of the head of the family at the moment of the referral.

Religious Beliefs

For many African American families, the church (particularly an African American church) is considered an important member of the extended family (Griffith, English, & Mayfield, 1980; Levin & Taylor, 1993). Therefore, an important guideline is to explore the role that the church plays in the life of an African American client. An initial approach is to determine the client's particular church affiliation. Examples of church affiliation generally reported by African American clients include Baptist, African Methodist Episcopal, Jehovah's Witness, Church of God in Christ, Seventh Day Adventist, Pentecostal, Apostolic, Presbyterian, Lutheran, Episcopal, Roman Catholic, and Nation of Islam. The majority of African American clients belong to the Baptist and the African Methodist Episcopal churches (Boyd-Franklin, 1989).

Despite the central role that the church plays in the lives of many African Americans (Smith, 1981), the therapist must avoid the generalization of this point across all African American clients seen in therapy. A second approach is to explore whether the particular client includes the church in his or her extended family. One way to investigate this is to ask "Have you discussed your emotional problems with someone in your church?" "Some-one" could be anybody (e.g., a friend, a minister, a priest). If church members are essential in providing instrumental and emotional support (according to the client), the therapist could ask, "Would you like to include these church members in our discussion of your concerns?"

Folk Beliefs

Some African American clients believe that folk medicine can be effective in the treatment of their medical and mental problems (Baker & Lightfoot, 1993; Wilkinson & Spurlock, 1986). Within the belief systems of many African Americans, mental problems can be the result of not only physical causes, but also occult or spiritual factors. If the illness has a physical cause, it could be cured with herbs, teas, and other natural substances and folk doctors are often consulted for treatment. If the illness is the result of occult or spiritual factors (including evil spirits, supernatural forces, violation of sacred beliefs, or sin), folk healers are consulted for treatment (Dana, 1993a).

When African American clients seek help for their mental health problems, four types of healers are often available. The old lady generally deals with common ailments, provides advice, gives medication (e.g., the use of herbs), and is most often consulted by young mothers. The spiritualist is the most common folk healer among African Americans seeking help. The voodoo priest or *hougan* has more formal training in the process of healing (including selecting plants for healing purposes, prescribing the ingestion of organs or parts of certain animals to treat the problem, and having the skills to deal with individual and family problems). In addition, many African American clients believe that the solution of their problems should include the client's involvement with Bible study groups, prayer meetings, and advice from a minister (Dana, 1993a). To enhance the assessment and treatment of African American clients, the therapist should accept these beliefs regarding the client's understanding of causation of mental health problems and their solution (Baker & Lightfoot, 1993; Smith, 1981).

Healthy Paranoia

Slavery and racism are two important factors in the history of African Americans in the United States that have dramatically shaped the social and psychological development of this group over time (Smith, 1981). An important consequence of these factors is the development of the *healthy cultural paranoia* phenomenon (Ho, 1992; Smith, 1981). African Americans present themselves as highly suspicious of others with different colors and values; this could interfere with the client-therapist relationship. If the therapist perceives that the client does not trust him or her and requests explanation for this healthy cultural paranoia instead of demonstrating an understanding of this phenomenon in historical terms, the client may perceive the therapist as culturally insensitive.

The Language of African American Clients

Communicative exchange between the client and therapist is an essential element in the process of psychotherapy. This point applies to all forms of therapy and not only to those therapies termed "talk therapy." Communicative exchange could be difficult to fulfill when the client uses words, sentences, a syntax, and phonology that are not part of the language of the therapist (Wilkinson & Spurlock, 1986). This point is particularly important to remember in the assessment and treatment of African American clients who may use Black English (instead of Standard American English) or street talk during the therapeutic process. Practitioners are encouraged to consult Dillard (1973), who provides a wide variety of examples demonstrating that distinction.

For example, in terms of grammar, the question "Have they gone there" (Standard American English) would be replaced by "Is they gone there?" in Black English (Dillard, 1973, p. 49). In other cases, what is at issue is the meaning of the particular sentence. For example, if an African American mother reports "My child sick" and another African American mother reports "My child be sick," the meaning of the first sentence is that the child is currently sick and the sickness is of short-term duration; the second sentence, however, indicates that the child has been sick for a long time (Dillard, 1973).

The use of street talk is another point to consider in the assessment and treatment of African American clients. In this case, the speaker (i.e., the client) may or may not use Standard American English, but the listener (i.e., the therapist) may have problems understanding words or sentences used by the speaker. For example, the sentence "I would like to have a hog to see my chick, but I have no bread" is grammatically correct in Standard American English, but the listener will not understand this sentence unless he or she is familiar with the slang words "hog" (a Cadillac, and, more generally a car), "chick" (girl), and "bread" (money; Dillard, 1973, p. 240). Additional examples of street talk include "I was mad of her because she took my pick"—the word in question is "pick," which means comb; "If I get a gig, I will feel better" (gig means job); "My old lady died last year, but my old man is still alive" (old lady and old man mean parents); "He likes to rap with the dude who lives across the street" (rap means talk, dude means man).

The basic guideline is this: If a therapist cannot understand the language of an African American client, he or she should ask the client directly about what he or she does not understand (e.g., a word, the meaning of a sentence). Several African Americans consulted for this book reported that, in many instances, they also have problem understanding Black English and street talk. Thus therapists who cannot understand Black English or street talk should not feel embarrassed to ask questions to enhance communication between themselves and clients who use Black English or street talk. A variant of this guideline is that the African American client must understand that the therapist is not questioning the correctness of Black English (in comparison with Standard American English) or the particular word. The client must understand, both verbally and nonverbally, that the main goal of such questions or inquiries is to facilitate verbal exchanges (communication) between the therapist and the client, a crucial element in understanding the client's main concerns.

The First Session

The first session with any client sets the tone for a healthy client-therapist relationship in subsequent sessions (Baker, 1988; Ho, 1992; Smith, 1981). The literature suggests specific guidelines dealing with the use of cultural skills during the first encounter between an African American client and a therapist.

Discuss Racial Differences

Because of the history of racism and discrimination by the dominant Anglo American culture, an African American client referred to an Anglo American therapist might come to the first session with the belief that the therapist is an "alien" and that he or she will not be able to understand the problem because of racial differences. To minimize these feelings, the first thing that a therapist should do during the first session is to acknowledge that difference and encourage the client to talk about his or her feelings concerning this issue. Racial issues, however, should not be discussed during brief or emergency interventions involving a crisis (Wilkinson & Spurlock, 1986).

In those cases when the therapist is white and the client is African American, a suggested approach is for the therapist to say, "Some African American clients feel uncomfortable when they are referred to a white therapist. Perhaps we could briefly talk about feelings you may have regarding our racial differences." A statement suggested by Boyd-Franklin (1989) is "How do you feel about working with a white therapist?" (p. 102). These general comments may not only reduce racial tension between the client and the therapist, but may also help the therapist seem less anxious, more comfortable, and more sensitive to the client's expectations and beliefs (Baker, 1988). In addition, when racial differences are openly discussed with African American clients, the therapist may give the impression that the client can discuss anything in a safe environment.

Another important guideline is to avoid discussion of racial issues in subsequent sessions (unless the client brings them to the attention of the therapist). If a repetition of similar issues continues after the first session, the therapist may convey to the client the impression that he or she is anxious about the potential effects of cross-racial issues and that this anxiety may interfere with the ability of the therapist to assess and treat the client effectively (Boyd-Franklin, 1989).

Why Should an African American
Therapist Discuss Racial Issues
With an African American Client?

In those cases when the client and the therapist are African Americans, the assumption is that because of this shared racial status, the client will be less suspicious and guarded, more relaxed, and more open to discussing personal problems with the therapist. Thus it appears unnecessary to recommend a discussion of racial issues. However, this conclusion may not be completely true (Boyd-Franklin, 1989; Wilkinson & Spurlock, 1986). Boyd-Franklin (1989) points out that because of the "macho" belief among many African Americans, a client from this group may find it difficult to openly discuss personal matters in front of an African American therapist. In addition, an African American client treated by a therapist from the same race could also "check out" the therapist (i.e., pay attention to nonverbal cues suggesting that the therapist is distancing himself or herself from the client) and display the same healthy cultural paranoia assumed in those cases when an African American client is seen by a white therapist.

One important guideline for an African American therapist treating an African American client is to avoid thinking that racial similarity will necessarily enhance (or guarantee) the therapist-client therapeutic relationship. The therapist should present a set of verbal and nonverbal behaviors leading to the establishment of himself or herself as a peer, rather than assuming that the client will consider the therapist a peer simply because he or she is African American. A useful statement to indicate that the therapist is interested in discussing racial issues with a client from the same race is "African Americans sometimes feel uncomfortable discussing mental problems with African American mental health professionals. Because I am African American [or black, depending on the client's preference of the terms], I wonder if you feel the same way with me?" To facilitate a verbal exchange between the client and the therapist regarding this issue, the therapist should avoid sitting behind a desk to signal to the client that the therapist does not want to distance himself or herself from the client and to convey the sense that discussion of racial issues will be taken very seriously. This physical arrangement is recommended throughout the entire process of therapy to continue the development of trust between the client and the therapist (Boyd-Franklin, 1989).

It is important to make a distinction between a discussion of racial issues to facilitate assessment and treatment during the first session and the therapist's (explicit or implicit) role as a "protector of the race" (Boyd-Franklin 1989). African Americans are aware of their history of rejection, racism, and slavery in the United States. Thus an African American client may become suspicious of African American therapists who, in the process of assessment and treatment, present themselves as members of this race with the education and training to "preach and teach" African American clients. Therefore, in addition to scheduling a brief period to discuss racial issues, it is also important to avoid mixing discussion of racial issues leading to the development of the therapeutic relationship with discussions involving political or racial problems in society.

Regardless of the race of the therapist a discussion of racial differences during the first therapy session does not necessarily guarantee the enhancement of the therapist-client relationship in subsequent sessions. As noted by Wilkinson and Spurlock (1986), "the therapist's openness, sensitivity, and ability . . . training and experience, are generally more important" (p. 51).

Explore the Level
of Acculturation

The fact that a client is an African American does not mean that the client feels that way (Dana, 1993a; Ho, 1992). Some African American clients prefer to identify with the Anglo American culture and may display behavior patterns like those displayed by the Anglo American community (e.g., dressing, music, language). This preference may be acquired through the process of internal acculturation, which should be explored to determine an African American client's perception of identity with the dominant culture versus the client's perception of racial identity with his or her own race (Sue & Sue, 1990). One way to explore this point is by encouraging the client to talk about his or her past and current experiences with the African American community versus his or her experiences with the Anglo American community. In addition, the Brief Acculturation Scale described in Chapter 2 (Figure 2.1) may be useful.

Avoid Causal Explanations of Problems

In general, African American clients believe that emotional problems are caused by environmental factors. Thus linking the mental health problem with parents' behavior (or with that of other members of the extended family) is not a good tactic when working with African American clients. The best approach would be to avoid explanation regarding the origin of the problem during the first session. During this session, African American clients generally prefer concrete suggestions regarding the solution of their problems, rather than long and complex explanations about the origin of these problems (Baker, 1988).

Include the Church in the Assessment and Therapy Processes

The church plays a major role in the life of African Americans (Griffith et al., 1980; Taylor & Chatters, 1986). This observation is particularly important to remember in the assessment and treatment of African American women, because they tend to show more involvement with church activities than African American men (Levin & Taylor, 1993). A practical guideline is to assess whether the client is a member of a particular church and the availability of economic and emotional supports from the particular church. The next step is to inform the client that he or she may bring church members to subsequent meetings to help with the assessment and treatment of the client's concerns (e.g., "If you believe that someone in your church should be invited to discuss this problem with you and me, please let me know and I will be glad to extend an invitation to that person"). If, prior to the first meeting, the therapist is aware (e.g., through information given by the client on the phone when scheduling the first meeting) that the client belongs to one of the churches in the community, the client should be told either on the phone or in writing that he or she may bring any church member to the first meeting. It is also important to inform the staff (e.g., secretaries, mental health paraprofessionals) about this guideline, because in many instances the therapist is not the person making the first contact with an African American when he or she calls the clinic to make an appointment.

With African American clients who are new residents in the community, the therapist should explore if the client has already found a church that could fulfill his or her religious needs. The therapist should be familiar with the churches available in that particular community. A good approach is to have a listing with the name, phone number, and address for each church that can be made available to new African American residents. As noted by Boyd-Franklin (1989), helping an African American client find a church may play a significant role in the process of psychotherapy (e.g., the minister may help in encouraging the client to come back for therapy or to follow the therapist's recommendations). In addition, this sort of assistance may greatly enhance the therapist-client therapeutic relationship.

Define the Role of Those
Accompanying the Client

Many African Americans bring members of the extended family (biological and nonbiological members) to the initial interview because they expect that the therapist will allow the presence of such members during that interview (Baker, 1988). These members often include relatives (uncles, aunts) and nonrelatives (friends, godfather, church members). To avoid making false assumptions about the role of these people during the first session, the therapist should clarify that role prior to the assessment of the case. The main concern here is to determine situations in which these extended family members could help in the evaluation and treatment of the client (Griffith & Baker, 1993). This guideline is particularly important to remember in those cases when the grandmother comes to the first meeting. The grandmother is probably the second most important member of the extended family (behind the church) in the African American community (Boyd-Franklin, 1989). Thus the presence of the grandmother in the first meeting is often a sign of social and/or spiritual support.

In many African American families, the primary caretaker is not the mother but the grandmother. If the grandmother brings a child for assessment and treatment, however, she may show a lack of understanding of fundamental psychological and developmental processes relevant in the assessment and treatment of the child. Despite this lack of understanding, the grandmother makes major decisions regarding the child's life. Thus the therapist should expect that the mother may not follow recommendations for assessment and treatment without the approval of the grandmother. For this reason, an important guideline to consider in the assessment and treatment of African American children is for the therapist to explore the role of the grandmother in the child's life in the first session. If the therapist perceives that this role is crucial, the grandmother should be invited to attend subsequent therapy sessions and to participate actively in the assessment and treatment of the case.

Use a Present-Time Focus

During the first session, an African American client will discuss both the core or most essential problem he or she feels should be considered first and additional problems that may be handled in later sessions (Baker, 1988). For the core problem, the client would expect the therapist to suggest a focused, brief intervention to deal with that problem quickly.

Screen Carefully for Depression

Griffith and Baker (1993) suggest that the myth that African Americans cannot become depressed could result in the underdiagnosis of depression in this group. These authors recommend screening the following criteria before concluding that an African American client does not have major depression.

- Neurovegetative signs (e.g., weight loss, fatigue)
- Client's view of the future
- Past and current sources of pleasures from specific persons
- Level of productivity
- Degree of participation in church activities
- Degree of participation as caregivers for younger family members

Avoid Misdiagnosing Substance
Abuse Syndromes as Schizophrenia

Griffith and Baker (1993) also note that the high prevalence of schizophrenia reported among African Americans may be the result of a history of substance abuse in this group. Hallucinations and delusions are the key symptoms in a diagnosis of schizophrenia. However, these symptoms can also result from chronic alcoholism or the use of illicit drugs (e.g., cocaine, heroin, cocaine derivative, crack). Thus during the first session with an African American client the therapist should screen for a history of substance abuse. If this client comes to the clinic with symptoms of schizophrenia and these symptoms disappear within approximately 2 hours in the absence of treatment (e.g., medication), the client probably has experienced a cocaine psychosis. In this case, failure to screen for substance abuse would lead to an error in diagnosing that client with schizophrenia.

Handle Family Secrets With Care

During the first session with an African American client, the therapist must be sensitive to the possibility of family secrets. The therapist should wait for the natural revelation of these secrets over time, because in most cases that revelation is simply a matter of timing (Boyd-Franklin, 1989). Family secrets can take many forms, including reasons for adoption (i.e., why the child was adopted by his aunt), use of drugs by parents (and other members of the family), past problems with the police leading to arrest and conviction, and secrets regarding fatherhood (Boyd-Franklin, 1989).

There are specific guidelines in the literature regarding methods to identify these secrets during the first session, as well as general guidelines concerning appropriate ways to handle these secrets. For example, if a grandmother brings a child to the clinic and she states that she has adopted the child without providing a reason for the adoption, the therapist may suspect a family secret. If an adolescent asks her parents in the presence of the therapist, "Why do I look different from my sisters?" and the therapist senses that the parents avoid the question, this could be a case of family secrets. If the therapist says, "Mr. Brown, could you tell me about your life when you were an adolescent?" and he replies, "I don't feel like talking about this now," another family secret might be suspected.

The basic guideline in the identification of suspected family secrets includes three elements: listen carefully to what the client says; attend to the amount of silence when the client is questioned about an issue that appears to be sensitive; and do not ask questions that may imply the revelation of family secrets. For example, during the first session, practitioners generally expect parents to be present to register a child and sign documents dealing with consent for assessment and treatment. If a parent is not present to fulfill this task, it would be inappropriate to ask a grandparent, an adult brother or sister, or an adult aunt or uncle, "Why isn't Sue's mother here today?" This question may seem appropriate to the therapist, but could be an invitation to discuss a secret prematurely, and the result could be attrition (i.e., the family may not come back for additional sessions).

In this circumstance, three steps are recommended. First, the therapist should inquire about the relationship between the child and the person(s) seeking help for the child (e.g., a grandparent) to determine the person's legal guardian status. Second, the therapist should clearly state that if that person is not the legal guardian, the child will be seen to determine if there is an emergency that requires immediate attention (e.g., suicide attempts). If the person states that he or she is not the legal guardian, the following comment is suggested: "I am very pleased that you brought Sue to this clinic today, which shows that you care about her. I will see Sue to determine that she is not danger to herself or to others. In the next session, it would be helpful if you could bring Sue's legal guardian to sign consent for further assessment and therapy." This statement not only avoids questions dealing with family secrets, but it also provides that person with the opportunity to mention the child's legal guardian without pressure from the therapist. The third step is for the therapist to be familiar with state laws and regulations regarding consent in the assessment and treatment of children and adolescents. For example, in Texas a family member (e.g., a grandparent, an adult brother or sister) may consent for the treatment of a child "when the person having the power to consent . . . cannot be contacted and actual notice to the contrary has not been given by that person" (Costello & Hays, 1988, p. 87).

Do Not Try "Hard" to Understand African American Clients

In a workshop dealing with the assessment and treatment of African American clients, presenters made the following recommendation: "If you try hard to understand African Americans, then you do not understand them at all." The same suggestion can be found in Boyd-Franklin (1989). For example, an Anglo therapist may use slang words that he or she believes are representative of African American dialect. The intention of the therapist would be to make an "attempt to join with the [African American] family" (Boyd-Franklin, 1989, p. 100). This approach, however, is not recommend with African American clients for two reasons: The therapist may use slang in an inappropriate context, and this approach may be considered by clients as condescending.

Do Not Emphasize Deficits;
Emphasize Strengths

During the first session with an African American client, it is important to avoid any suggestion (either verbal or nonverbal) leading to the assumption that the client comes from a disorganized, unstable, or psychologically unhealthy family because of the client's color. This characterization of African American families was the prevalent view during the 1960s; it has been challenged in the last 20 years. For example, the assumption that a stable, organized, and psychologically healthy family "must consist of two parents" (Boyd-Franklin, 1989, p. 15) suggests that any family lacking this attribute is inherently pathological. Because this attribute is not shared by many African American families (many of which are headed by single mothers), the conclusion would be that these families are disorganized, unstable, and psychologically unhealthy. This conclusion is not only untrue (Wilkinson & Spurlock, 1986), but it also does not take into consideration the role of other factors (e.g., the role of the extended family, role flexibility, strong religious orientation, and strong emphasis on the value of education) that can lead to normal functioning in families headed by a single parent. These factors are the strengths of the African American family, which the therapist should emphasize and use in subsequent sessions to encourage African American families to participate in therapy (Boyd-Franklin, 1989).

In the case of the role of the extended family, many African American mothers report during the first session that they are single mothers. If the therapist does not explore further the definition of extended family in the mind of the client, the role of a stepfather may not be revealed in the first session. The stepfather may play an essential role in the development and maintenance of family functioning during the process of psychotherapy, but this role will not be revealed until the therapist explores the impact of the extended family (as defined in Chapter 2).

Conducting Psychotherapy

The above guidelines are recommended during the first therapeutic contact with African American clients, in which the emphasis is placed upon the collection of preliminary clinical data, with minimal emphasis on the psychotherapy process. If the client returns for psychotherapy in subsequent sessions (Chapter 7 summarizes guidelines to prevent attrition from therapy), another set of guidelines are recommended (Baker, 1988;

Boyd-Franklin, 1989; Dana, 1993a; Griffith & Baker, 1993; Ho, 1992, 1993; Lefley & Pedersen, 1986; Smith, 1981).

Emphasize Empowerment

During the course of therapy with an African American client, it is important to reinforce the concept of empowerment and to relate this concept to the client's experience with therapeutic changes. This concept is important with any family regardless of cultural background. In the case of African American clients, however, the concept plays an especially important role because of a long history of slavery, racism, and discrimination experienced by this group in the United States. Two major goals of a therapist when dealing with that concept in psychotherapy are to help the client gain the skills necessary to make important decisions in his or her own life and the life of the family (including children, wife, extended family members) and to assist the client in the development of skills that could help the client to take control of his or her family.

For example, an African American client may experience a sense of powerlessness because in his or her mind he or she does not have the right to select a therapist in those cases when the client is referred for therapy by a welfare agency. In this example, the therapist's task is to be sensitive to that sense of powerlessness (e.g., "I understand that you feel that you cannot make a decision regarding the selection of a therapist") and to make clear that specific techniques to develop skills to deal with these feeling will be discussed during the process of psychotherapy (e.g., the use of problem-solving and social-skill training to reestablish power).

Recommended Modalities of Therapy With African American Clients

Problem-Solving and Social-Skills Training

The central goal of problem-solving training is to teach people to deal quickly with the solution of one or more problems in a series of problems (Kratochwill & Bergan, 1990). Because the therapist teaches the client how to resolve his or her own problems when problem-solving techniques are used, this strategy may be perceived by the client as a way of taking power (or control) over his or her own behavior or over other family members. In general, African American clients (and other multicultural groups) expect a quick solution to problems they identify as essential (among a set of target problems). As these problems are identified and solved with problem-solving techniques, the development of credibility (e.g., the feeling that the therapist knows what to do with this particular client and his or her problems) and a sense of trust toward the therapist are facilitated (Boyd-Franklin, 1989).

Teaching clients to be assertive by using appropriate social skills is the main goal of social-skills training (Lange & Jakubowski, 1976). As noted by Yamamoto et al. (1993), many members of culturally diverse groups "feel they cannot speak up or assert themselves. Despite improving race relations, [diverse groups] often express that they still feel as if they are second-class citizens" (p. 116). Social-skills training is recommended with African American clients who are not assertive in their interpersonal relationships (including with family members) because of fear of negative consequences (rejection, verbal reprimands) or because they believe they do not have the right to express their reactions to other people with "power" outside the extended family.

Family Therapy

As noted above, the extended family plays a major role in the life of many African American clients. For this reason, several authors suggest that family therapy should be considered among the first treatment approaches with African American clients (Boyd-Franklin, 1989, pp. 141-142). All forms of family therapy are recommended. Two tactics are recommended with any form of family therapy scheduled with African American families (Boyd-Franklin, 1989, pp. 141-142). The first tactic is an emphasis on the assignment of tasks that the family should conduct at home and report to the therapist in subsequent sessions. This tactic not only allows the therapist to deal with the solution of the problem in the target setting (e.g., at home), but it may also encourage other family members (who refuse to come to family therapy) to participate (or to be more active) in the process of family therapy. In addition, because many African American clients enter treatment looking for a "quick fix" of their problems (Boyd-Franklin, 1989), the assignment of tasks could be seen by these clients as an example of the therapist's interest in quickly dealing with the problem.

The second tactic is the scheduling of role-play scenarios to develop communication among family members. Many African American clients are not familiar with the concept of family therapy as something that can actually help them solve their problems. Several family therapy sessions are recommended to encourage each family member to role play the way he or she might talk about the target problem at home and how all members could find solutions to that particular problem when they elect to communicate their feelings and concerns to other family members. One important consequence of role playing in family therapy with African Americans is that this tactic could enhance the therapist's ability to reestablish the sense of power or control in the family. By learning how to communicate and solve problems in role-playing scenarios, an African American client may also learn that the "powerlessness" and "weakness" he or she experienced prior to family therapy could be transformed into a sense of empowerment or control. Boyd-Franklin (1989) suggests that the reestablishment of this sense of control should be seen as a fundamental task in the treatment of African American clients.

When the goal of family therapy is to deal with emotional problems among couples, additional guidelines are recommended. In general, when white couples seek help from a therapist, both partners agree to discuss their problems with the therapist. As noted by Boyd-Franklin (1989), this level of agreement "is exceedingly rare among [African American] people" (p. 225). Boyd-Franklin suggests that this observation could be explained in terms of the socialization of African American men, in which the impact of racism, discrimination, and the development of the macho role prevents men from showing weakness during difficult times. These factors in the process of socialization of African American men could have major implications in relationships between African American men and women. The admission of emotional problems and reports about these problems to people outside the family network (e.g., the therapist) may be interpreted as a sign of weakness in the mind of many African American men.

Thus, assuming that the man comes to the first family therapy session, a major problem that the therapist may have to confront during subsequent sessions is to determine strategies to encourage the man to come back for therapy. Body-Franklin (1989) provides a series of general guidelines for engaging African American men in family therapy. First, the therapist should signal to the woman that she could be seen alone. Second, the therapist should explore the woman's understanding of her partner's position with respect to therapy for their mutual problems. Third, although the woman may give the man an ultimatum (e.g., "If you do not come to therapy, I will leave you"), it is important for the therapist to inform the woman that this approach may signal to the man that he is being forced to come to therapy, and that as a result of this "forced-choice" tactic the man may feel that he may lose his autonomy and the power to choose his own ways of confronting and resolving the problem. Fourth, it is important for the woman to understand that it may help if the therapist talks to the man directly. A time and day when the man could be reached on the phone should be determined in the first session and the woman should be instructed to inform her partner that the therapist will call him at that particular time. The therapist should emphasize that he or she wants to talk to the man directly instead of using the woman as the messenger. Because of the generally negative attitude toward therapy and the cultural paranoia among African Americans, during the first phone conversation with the man the therapist must tell him that he or she has discussed the problem with the man's partner and that the main purpose of the present conversation is to explore his ideas, suggestions, or understanding with respect to the target problem (only the problem mentioned by the woman to the therapist). The therapist should also emphasize that this information is needed to assist (avoid the term "help") the couple in the solution of their concerns (avoid the term "problem").

4

Guidelines for the Assessment and Treatment of Hispanics

The second largest multicultural group in U.S. mental health services is Hispanic. In 1991, the total number of Hispanics was approximately 21.4 million (U.S. Bureau of the Census, 1992). The majority of Hispanics were Mexican Americans (approximately 13.4 million), Puerto Ricans (2.3 million), and Cubans (1.0 million). It is estimated that by 2020, 47 to 54.3 million Hispanics will be residing in the United States (Dana, 1993a; Marin & Marin, 1991). The majority of Hispanics (approximately 86%) in the United States live in urban areas (Marin & Marin, 1991).

In summarizing data from the 1982 U.S. Census, Marin and Marin (1991) note that the majority of four subgroups of Hispanics (Mexican Americans, Cubans, Puerto Ricans, and Dominicans) reside in four states: California (31.1%), Texas (20.4%), New York (11.4%), and Florida (5.9%). Most Mexican Americans live in southwestern states (Arizona, California, Colorado, New Mexico, and Texas). The majority of Cubans live in Florida (mainly in Miami); the majority of Puerto Ricans and Dominicans live in the New York and New Jersey areas. Other Hispanics from Central America (e.g., Panama, Costa Rica, Nicaragua) and South America (e.g., Colombia, Venezuela) reside mostly in New York City and San Francisco (Marin & Marin, 1991).

In 1991, the median income for Hispanic families (including Mexican Americans, Cubans, Puerto Ricans, Central and South American Hispanics, and other Hispanics) was $23,431, below the national median of $35,353 and in comparison with $36,915 for white families (U.S. Bureau of the Census, 1992). It should be noted that in 1991 the median income for Hispanics was slightly higher than the median income for African Americans ($21,423). Among the larger subgroups of Hispanics in the United States, Cubans reported the highest median income level in 1991 ($31,439) and Puerto Ricans reported the lowest level ($18,008). In 1991, approximately 25.0% of Hispanic families and 28.1% of Hispanic persons were below the poverty level, in comparison with 8.1% of white families and 10.7% of white persons. Cubans reported the lowest percentage of families below the poverty level in 1991—13.8% (U.S. Bureau of the Census, 1992).

Terminology

In general, a person is considered "Hispanic" in terms of language skill (Spanish speaking), family name (Spanish surname), or ancestry (Spanish American). Ruiz and Padilla (1977) use the concept of Hispanics to include all persons of "Spanish origin and descent." A more inclusive definition of Hispanics is provided by Marin and Marin (1991): "individuals who reside in the United States and who were born in or trace the background of their families to one of the Spanish-speaking Latin American nations or Spain" (p. 1). These persons include people from Spain, Central American countries (e.g., Mexico, Panama, Costa Rica), South American countries (e.g., Venezuela, Colombia), and the Caribbean (e.g., Puerto Rico, Cuba).

Two additional terms commonly used are "Latino" and "Hispanic American." Latino implies that a person is from a Latin American country; as noted by Dana (1993a), Mexican Americans tend to prefer this term because it "does not signify the conqueror Spain" (p. 66). Hispanic American implies that a person is not only of Spanish origin but that he or she was born in the United States. Currently, the literature suggests that most investigators prefer the term Hispanic in its most general sense (Dana, 1993a; Ho, 1992; Marin & Marin, 1991; Ruiz, 1981), including people who label themselves as Hispanics because they are from Spain, from any of the South American or Central American nations, or from the Caribbean. Because many people who consider themselves Hispanic do not speak Spanish, it may not be appropriate to label a person Hispanic on the basis of the ability to speak Spanish.

Cultural Variables That May
Affect Assessment and Treatment

Religious and Folk Beliefs

For Hispanics, religious and folk beliefs are similar to those found among African American clients (Dana, 1993a; Ho, 1992; C. Martinez, 1993). The priest is a key figure in the process of understanding and assisting Hispanics in solving their problems. Hispanic clients may believe that mental health problems are caused by evil spirits and, as a result, the church, not the therapist, has the power to treat these problems. Hispanics often believe that prayers will cure a physical or mental health problem, and help from a mental health professional is often sought when the family has exhausted all religious and folk resources to handle the problem. Certain forms of behavior such as *envidia* (envy) and *mal de ojo* (evil eye), which is said to result from excessive admiration and attention, might result in physical and mental health problems in others. The *espiritista* (spiritualist), *el curandero* (for men) or *la curandera* (for women) (folk healer), or *el brujo* or *la bruja* (witch doctor) can be consulted to resolve these problems. Knowledge concerning these beliefs among Hispanic communities enhances the assessment and treatment of Hispanic clients.

Machismo, Respeto, and *Marianismo*

In general, men tend to be the dominant authority in a Hispanic family, including exercising direct sexual power over women. Qualities that are collectively known as *machismo* include physical strength, sexual attractiveness, masculinity, aggressiveness, and the ability to consume an excessive amount of alcohol without getting drunk (Comas-Díaz, 1988; Comas-Díaz & Duncan, 1985). Among Hispanic men, *machismo* also denotes a sense of *respeto* (respect) from others. As noted by Comas-Díaz and Duncan (1985), the term *respeto* generally "dictates the appropriate deferential behavior toward others on the basis of age, social position, economic status, and sex" (p. 465).

In the context of *machismo, respeto* is seen as an example of submission by others (e.g., children and wife) to the authority of a man. In the context of interpersonal relationships, a Hispanic who shows *respeto* for authority (parents, elders) is considered *una persona bien educada* (a well-educated person). This person has been taught by his or her parents the importance of demonstrating social relationships *con respeto* (with respect) and *dig-*

nidad (dignity). Therefore, if a child is called *mal educado* (without education), the implicit assumption in the Hispanic community is that this child did not receive education from his or her parents concerning the treatment of others (particularly persons in a position of authority) with *respeto*. As noted by Ho (1992), in the Hispanic community an individual "could be illiterate and still be considered *una persona bien educada*" (p. 108) if that person has good skills in human relationships and is able to show *respeto* in the presence of others (particularly authority, such as parents and elders).

Thus, if during the intake process a Hispanic father reports that "*Mi hijo no tienes educación*" (my son does not have education), this statement means that his son does not show respect to him and other people with authority. A therapist unfamiliar with this issue would emphasize a line of questioning dealing with the son's school performance rather than further screening of *respeto*.

In the case of *marianismo*, women are expected to be submissive, obedient, dependent, timid, docile, sentimental, gentle, and to remain a virgin until marriage (Comas-Díaz, 1988; Comas-Díaz & Duncan, 1985; Martinez, 1988; Ruiz, 1981). Women are also expected to take care of children at home and to devote their time to cooking, cleaning the house, and doing other activities for the benefit of their children and husband. *Marianismo* is based on the Catholic worship of the Virgin Mary, who is considered among Hispanics as both a virgin and a madonna (Comas-Díaz & Duncan, 1985). In a general sense, *marianismo* means that women are not only spiritually superior to men, but they are the individuals who endure all suffering produced by men (Comas-Díaz, 1988; Comas-Díaz & Duncan, 1985).

When Hispanics move from their country of origin (where *machismo* and *marianismo* are socially accepted) to the United States (where *machismo* and *marianismo* are not socially accepted), an attempt to retain the qualities of *machismo* and *marianismo* may lead to conflicts among family members (e.g., marital problems between husband and wife, child-father conflicts). In this circumstance, the most practical approach would be to avoid changing those beliefs during psychotherapy and, instead, to present concrete examples leading to the client's understanding of why such beliefs are not socially accepted in the United States.

Familismo

Among Hispanics, the family relationship is paramount (Ho, 1992; Ruiz, 1981). Thus any attempt to conduct psychotherapy without the involvement of the client's family (including nuclear and extended family) is the route to failure. Hispanics generally turn to family members during times of stress and economic difficulties, and often consult with other members in the family before they decide to seek help from a therapist. This is particularly true in the case of more traditional Hispanic families, in comparison with more acculturated families (Comas-Díaz, 1994). Consultation sometimes involves members from the extended family network who are not related to the family by blood or marriage, such as the godfather (*padrino*), godmother (*madrina*), and friends, but are tied to the family through special relationships.

Role flexibility is not rewarded in Hispanic communities. The father is the head of the family, the wife takes care of the children, and children must behave according to the father's rules.

Personalismo

In general, Hispanics are more oriented toward people than toward impersonal relationships (Bernal & Gutierrez, 1988; Ho, 1992; C. Martinez, 1993). This phenomenon is known as *personalismo* (personalism). In general, Hispanics feel uncomfortable when they are treated as "things" or "abstractions." This feeling could extend to perceiving that the distance between a speaker (e.g., the client) and a listener (e.g., the therapist) is wide, sensing a lack of "warmth" because one is not hugged when shaking hands with someone else (e.g., the therapist), or feeling that someone avoids sharing personal information.

Personalismo could indirectly affect a Hispanic's selection of a therapist and the process of psychotherapy. Many Hispanic clients might select a therapist not on the basis of professional credentials but on the basis of the therapist's ability to disclose personal information (excluding intimate aspects of the therapist's life) such as food preferences, music, and hobbies, that enable the client to develop a certain level of trust and confidence in the therapist. However, this observation may not apply in the case of Hispanics with professional status who, in addition to personalism, also tend to look for professional credentials when seeking help from mental health professionals (Comas-Díaz, 1994).

Another expression of *personalismo* during the process of psychotherapy is the offering of gifts or presents by Hispanic clients as a way of expressing gratitude and generosity for the services provided by the therapist. Systematic rejection of such gifts may hurt the client's feeling of *personalismo*, which in turn could result in the client dropping out from therapy. Therapists working with Hispanic clients need to recognize and acknowledge the conditions under which it is culturally appropriate to accept such gifts (e.g., during Christmas, the therapist may receive from a Mexican American client a wooden cup made in Mexico) and those conditions under which it may be clinically appropriate to reject the gift (e.g., receiving the wooden cup as a form of payment for therapy).

Individualismo

American individualism emphasizes competition among people leading to an individual's ability to obtain economic and professional success without the assistance of other members of the community (Sandoval & De La Roza, 1986). In the case of Hispanics, *individualismo* (individualism) emphasizes what is unique about each member of the community and how this uniqueness leads to cooperation rather than to competition (Canino & Canino, 1993). *Individualismo* means that everyone has something to offer to the Hispanic community. This offering is the individual's peculiarity, which makes him or her unique in comparison with other members of the community, such as particular job skills or cooking skills.

Among many Hispanics, *individualismo* and *familismo* are related, in that an individual's own peculiarities are expected to be shared by all members of the family (e.g., mother's ability to cook traditional Hispanic dishes is shared by all family members). The sense of *individualismo* should be explored in the assessment and treatment of Hispanic clients. This is particularly recommended in cases when the client feels or perceives that the therapist's suggestions for changing behaviors means that the client's sense of *individualismo* could be jeopardized.

Fatalismo

Believing that a divine providence governs the world and that an individual cannot control or prevent adversity is an example of Hispanics' sense of *fatalismo* (fatalism) (Ho, 1992; Neff & Hoppe, 1993). Among Hispanics, fatalism might be interpreted at least in two ways. Fatalism could imply a sense of vulnerability and lack of control in the presence of adverse events, as well as the feeling that such events are "waiting" to affect the life of the individual. This belief could negatively affect the treatment of Hispanic clients, particularly in cases when the goals of therapy compete with the client's perception that no protection exists against problems with roots in fatalism. Fatalism may also be interpreted in terms of an adaptive response to uncontrollable life situations (Neff & Hoppe, 1993). This sense of fatalism is often associated with the individual's involvement in religious activities, which provide both personal and social resources for the individual.

In the treatment of a fatalistic Hispanic client, the therapist should carefully screen which form of fatalism applies to that client. If the client is fatalistic in accordance with the first form of fatalism, it would be appropriate to encourage that client to be involved in religious activities to minimize the negative impact of fatalism (in the sense of lack of control in the presence of adverse events) on the treatment process (Neff & Hoppe, 1993).

Perception of Skin Color

In the United States, the terms "black" and "white" constitute the major racial denominations. Among Hispanics, a wide range of racial denominations exists (Ramos-McKay, Comas-Díaz, & Rivera, 1988). This observation is particularly true in the case of Puerto Ricans, Cubans, and Dominicans. For example, dark-skinned persons are called *morenos* or *prietos*; those with olive skin or dark complexions are *trigueños*. Persons with light skin or kinky hair are known as *grifos*, *jabaos*, or *albinos*; people having Indian characteristics are called *indios*.

Among many Hispanics, membership in society is much more a function of class (e.g., low socioeconomic status versus high socioeconomic status) rather than color. Many Hispanics often say that "the green color is the most important color" (i.e., the color of a dollar). Thus Hispanics with a low socioeconomic status in their countries of origin believe that when they are discriminated against in their own country, it is because they belong to a class with little economic resources, regardless of their skin color. When Hispanics enter the United States, however, they experience a different sense of discrimination when they find out that skin color can be an important variable in the phenomenon of discrimination. For example, many *morenos* or *prietos* do not classify themselves as black (or African American). Yet, when these persons enter the United States, they find out that they are perceived as blacks. Because in many Hispanic families some members are *morenos* or *prietos* and other members are *grifos* or *jabaos* (resembling white skin color), such families experience an even more dramatic crisis of identity when they find out that some of their members are perceived as blacks and others are treated as whites in the United States.

Because many Hispanics do not emphasize skin color to make racial classifications, the therapist should avoid traditional race denominations during the process of assessment and treatment of Hispanic clients. The therapist should explore the client's preference of a given skin color in his or her family and how this preference may impact the assessment and treatment of the client. For example, some Hispanic parents (particularly Mexican Americans) prefer children with light skin color because such parents believe that "if one looks and acts European, one is more acceptable" (Ho, 1992, p. 105). As noted by Ho (1992), darker children raised in a family where skin color is an issue (with preference given to light-skinned persons) could have serious self-identity conflicts. A preference by parents in having children with light skin colors might be a function of acculturation (Ramirez, 1994). Thus it is also important for the therapist to conduct an assessment of acculturation (see Table 8.1) and to integrate this assessment into the overall assessment and treatment of the client.

Insanity Versus Mental Illness

As noted by Dana (1993a), many Hispanics believe that a mental disorder (*enfermedad mental*) is less severe than being insane (*estar loco*). In the first case, the person suffers from a *crisis nerviosa* or *ataque de nervios* (a nervous crisis). In the second case, the client shows a complete loss of control and/or withdrawal (e.g., schizophrenia and major depression) requiring hospitalization. Hispanics who perceive themselves as having an *enfermedad mental* would seek help from friends, relatives, and healers rather than from mental health professionals. Therefore when a family member brings his or her Hispanic relative to a clinic, that family member may consider the client *loco* in the sense that he or she is seriously disturbed.

The First Session

Several specific guidelines have been proposed to facilitate the first encounter between a Hispanic client and a therapist (Bernal & Gutierrez, 1988; Dana, 1993a; Ho, 1992; C. Martinez, 1988, 1993; Ramos-McKay, Comas-Díaz, & Rivera, 1988; Ruiz, 1981).

Explore the Level of Acculturation

An assessment of both internal and external processes of acculturation should be conducted during the first session with all Hispanic clients (Dana, 1993a; Ho, 1992; Ramirez, Paniagua, Linskey, & O'Boyle, 1993; Ramirez, Wassef, Paniagua, Linskey, & O'Boyle, 1994). The discrepancy in the degree or level of acculturation among family members may itself produce conflicts in the family, leading to problems. This is particularly true in those cases when the identified client is a child or an adolescent (Bernal & Gutierrez, 1988).

For example, many traditional Hispanic families believe that a female adolescent must introduce her boyfriend to her parents before dating can be allowed. Dating is sometimes a complex process, including the participation of parents or relatives. In the United States, this process of dating is not generally accepted by American adolescents. Thus an acculturated Hispanic female residing in New York City with a family with traditional (Hispanic) values of what constitutes dating would create a family problem when she behaves in a way different from that expected by her parents when dating a man in this country (see Bernal & Gutierrez, 1988, pp. 250-252, for an illustrative case). In this example, parents may report that their daughter "became very depressed" (including diminished interest or pleasure in most activities, significant weight loss, and suicidal ideation) when she was told that dating will not be allowed without formal approval from her parents. A therapist with experience with the Hispanic culture would quickly realize that in this case the girl is not meeting her parents' cultural expectations regarding dating. The girl is considered more acculturated to the American value of dating than her parents (Martinez, 1986). During the first session, the therapist should recommend that such a discrepancy between levels of acculturation be carefully explored before he or she gives advice regarding the solution of the family problem (which could actually be a cultural problem).

Another important traditional Hispanic value is the belief that women cannot have the same freedom and autonomy as men. The belief in *marianismo* and *machismo* is strongly reinforced among many Hispanic families (Comas-Díaz & Duncan, 1985). The process of acculturation, however, may change this belief; the therapist encounters the task of determining how to deal with family problems that appear to be driven by the process of acculturation. If during the first session a therapist recommends that a Hispanic wife should have the same freedom and independence as her (Hispanic) husband, this recommendation would be an error, which could lead to attrition, and a sign of lack of understanding of that particular value upon the family.

A guideline to handle the above examples (and other similar examples indicating the potential effect of acculturation in the manifestation of mental problems) would be to screen the processes of acculturation (as described in Chapter 2) in each member of the family. A summary of acculturation scales recommended with Hispanic clients is included in Chapter 8. In subsequent sessions, emphasis should be placed upon a general discussion involving the concept of acculturation and how the family interprets this concept. In fact, this discussion may serve as one of the basic elements of a treatment plan with emphasis on family therapy.

Formalismo Versus *Personalismo*

As noted above, many Hispanics expect *personalismo* in their relationships with other people, including personal contacts and personal attention. However, personalism should be avoided with Hispanic clients during the first session and emphasis should be placed on *formalismo*. Two strategies are recommended to signal to Hispanic clients that proper formal relationships will be considered and respected.

The first strategy is to avoid a first-name informal relationship during the first session. For example, the clinician should say, "Good morning, Mr. Garcia" instead of "Hi, Juan" to a Hispanic client who just arrived for his first session. If the clinician can communicate in Spanish, the form *usted* (formal "you") instead of *tu* (informal "you") should be used (Martinez, 1986). For example, the therapist should say to a Hispanic client, "Cómo esta usted?" (How are you?) instead of "Cómo estas tu?" Because "you" is used in English to mean both *usted* and *tu*, it may be difficult for a clinician to determine in which condition "you" would mean *usted* rather than *tu* when communicating in English. The solution to this difficulty is actually very easy to remember: Always use the client's last name and Mr. (Mr. Martinez), Mrs. (Mrs. Martinez), or Miss (Miss Martinez) before using "you." For example, a clinician would say "Mr. Martinez, you said that . . ." instead of "Juan, you said that . . . ." In the first case, the meaning of "you" would be *usted* in the client's interpretation of a formal relationship (which in that sentence is given by the use of the client's last name and the forms Mr., Mrs., or Miss). If the therapist can speak Spanish, he or she should address the client as *Señor* (Mr.), *Señora* (Mrs.), or *Señorita* (Miss). Among Hispanics, *Señor* is used with adult males regardless of marital status; *Señora* is generally used to address women who are married. A *Señorita* is a woman who is at least 15 years old, not married, and considered a *virgen* (i.e., without a history of a sexual relationship).

Other terms used by many Hispanics to identify the status of a family member within the nuclear or extended family are *Don* and *Doña*. *Don* may be used to identify a Hispanic man with social and economic resources beyond those shared by other members of the Hispanic community. For example, the owner of a farm would be called *Don* (e.g., *Don* Martinez). *Doña* is generally used to identified the wife of that man (e.g., *Doña* Martinez). In general, however, both terms are used as a sign of *mucho respeto* (very much respect) for elderly Hispanics, regardless of their socioeconomic status (e.g., younger members of the Hispanic community would call Mr. and Mrs. Martinez *Don* and *Doña* Martinez as a sign of respect, regardless of the socio or economic resources of Mr. and Mrs. Martinez).

The second strategy to indicate that proper formal amenities will be considered and respected during the first session is to emphasize a formal conversation that includes the use of the client's last name and the forms Mr., Mrs., Miss, and a content strictly related to the mental disorder mentioned by the client. Thus the following example is not recommended with a Hispanic client in the first session: "Hi, Juan. My understanding is that you feel sad and need help. By the way, Juan, my notes indicate that your birthday was last week. Did you have a good time?" The client may interpret these remarks as informal and unrelated to the main problem. Such remarks, however, are examples of "chatting" (*la platica*), expected by Hispanic clients after the proper formal amenities have been considered and respected (Martinez, 1986).

Explore the Client's Magical Explanation of Mental Problems

Many Hispanics believe that mental problems might be determined by bad spirits or witchcraft (hex). These clients also believe that such problems may be resolved with the assistance of an *espiritista* or a *curandero(a)* who may combine expertise in treating these unseen (negative) events with the expertise of mental health professionals (Martinez, 1986). Sometimes Hispanics do not want to acknowledge in the first session that they believe in spiritualism (Comas-Díaz, 1994). During this session, however, the therapist's ability to explore, understand, and accept the client's magical or spiritual explanatory model of mental problems is crucial for two reasons.

First, exploring, understanding, and accepting the client's magical or spiritual interpretation of mental disorders may enhance the therapeutic relationship during the actual process of psychotherapy. Second, the therapist may use the client's explanatory model to produce positive behavioral changes. For example, it would be appropriate to indicate to a Hispanic client who maintains such beliefs that in subsequent sessions the therapist will be pleased to invite the *espiritista* or *curandero(a)*. Because the *espiritista or curandero(a)* generally conducts session with a group (and rarely with individuals), this recommendation is particularly important when the therapist plans to conduct group therapy with Hispanic clients who share the same beliefs.

As noted by Martinez (1986), if a therapist plans to work with Hispanic clients it is not only important to understand these beliefs but, more importantly, the therapist must be "prepared to function within both systems" (p. 80): the folk belief and the scientific systems. An emphasis on the scientific explanation of mental problems would probably compete with beliefs among Hispanic clients regarding the role of spirits (*espiritos*) and the function of the *curanderos* in the solution of mental problems (Dana, 1993a; Ho, 1992).

If the therapist prefers to deal with the problem from a purely scientific perspective, he or she should refer the client to another practitioner with training (and interest) in the delivery of mental health services to Hispanic clients with emphasis upon both systems.

It should be noted that witch doctors or *brujos* (for men) or *brujas* (for women) are not used by Hispanics in the same way as *curanderos* (men) or *curanderas* (women) are used. In general, *brujos* or *brujas* use the power of the devil to resolve problems; *curanderos* or *curanderas* use the power of God, in a spiritual sense (Cuellar, 1994). This distinction should be kept in mind when communicating with Hispanic clients.

Interview the Father Alone

When the problem involves family conflicts in which children are considered (by parents) as the center of that problem, it is recommended that the therapist interview the father alone for a few minutes during the first session. This approach is a recognition of the father's authority. Because of the value that Hispanics attach to the father's authority, a brief meeting between the therapist and the father could signal to the family that the therapist is sensitive to cultural variables and that he or she is ready to respect and to support them during the course of therapy. However, this approach should not be used with an acculturated family, or else the mother or wife may perceive that she has been left out in the assessment and treatment of the client (Cuellar, 1994). An assessment of acculturation is highly recommended before using this particular guideline.

Give the Sense That Medication Could Be Recommended

Many Hispanic clients expect medication during the first session. The therapist must first explore whether the client believes that medication is an important treatment for his or her problem. If it is important and the therapist disagrees with the use of medication, the next step is to discuss the reasons for not using medication. This point must be discussed during the first session. If medication may be used later, the client should be informed about this possibility (Bernal & Gutierrez, 1988; Ramos-McKay et al., 1988).

A Tentative Solution to the
Presenting Problem Is Expected

During the first session, Hispanic clients expect a combination of assessment (what is the problem) and treatment (here is what should be done to deal with this problem). Hispanic clients expect some immediate help from the therapist and at least a tentative solution to their problems (Ho, 1992). Thus, at the end of the first session with a Hispanic client, it is important to provide suggestions or recommendations that the client can use to deal with the problem at home. Informing the client at the end of the first session that more information is needed before a therapeutic approach is recommended may lead to attrition.

Conducting Psychotherapy

The following guidelines are selected from Bernal and Gutierrez (1988), Comas-Díaz and Duncan (1985), Dana (1993a), Ho (1992), C. Martinez (1986, 1988, 1993), Ramos-McKay et al. (1988), and Ruiz (1981).

Talk About Spiritual Issues

With all forms of therapies, a Hispanic client tends to expect the therapist to talk about spiritual factors that could cause emotional problems (including the *susto* or a magical fright, the *mal puesto* or the hex, and the *mal de ojo* or evil eye). Hispanic clients' beliefs about spiritual issues and how these beliefs may control the way the client thinks and acts should be explored during the first session. When conducting psychotherapy in subsequent sessions, this information should be used to facilitate the assessment and treatment of clients holding these beliefs.

Use More *Personalismo* and
Less *Formalismo*

During the psychotherapy process, Hispanic clients expect less *formalismo* and more *personalismo*, including proximity, hand-shaking, and discussion of personal issues by the therapist. The therapist must remember that in the first contact with Hispanic clients, *personalismo* is not generally recommended.

Recommended Modalities of Therapy

Family Therapy

Family therapy should be considered as the first therapeutic approach with all Hispanic clients. This is particularly important to remember in the assessment and treatment of immigrant families. Most Hispanics prefer this therapy because it reinforces their view of *familismo* and extended family. Nonblood extended family members (e.g., friends, the *compadre* or cofather, the *comadre* or comother) should be expected to attend family therapy sessions. When the discrepancy in levels of acculturation among family members is relatively high (as measured by one or more of the acculturation scales listed in Chapter 8), the therapist should discuss these levels using examples that each family member can understand. When using these examples, the therapist should emphasize that "being acculturated" does not mean rejecting familism. For example, in the case of the acculturated daughter having family problems because of her approach to dating, the therapist could say to the parents, "Mr. and Mrs. Martinez, I understand your concerns. It may help, however, if we talk about the way adolescents date in this country and how this way of dating does not mean that a female adolescent (like your daughter) is not concerned about her family." Traditional values among Hispanic families and new values acquired by later generations should be discussed during family therapy.

Group Therapy

Group therapy is recommended with Hispanic clients, but it should emphasize a problem-focus approach. In addition, several guidelines are recommended that should be considered prior to the scheduling of group therapy with Hispanic clients (Martinez, 1986).

If the therapist is bilingual and decides to conduct group therapy in Spanish, he or she should remember that although the grammar of Spanish is generally shared by countries in which the native and official language is Spanish, there are many variants in the ways Spanish-speaking people use Spanish in daily conversations. Thus clients must be told that although group therapy will be conducted in Spanish, in some cases it will be necessary for the speaker to explain the meaning of a word, phrase, or sentence that appears difficult to understand by other members of the group.

A client should not be included in that (Spanish-speaking) group simply because he or she is Hispanic (Martinez, 1986). Acculturated Hispanics may have problems understanding Spanish simply because they do not use their native language or have not used it for a long time. Thus it is important to screen the level of acculturation to determine the impact that language would have upon some members of the group (see Figure 2.1).

Clients sharing the same level of acculturation should be included in the same group (Martinez, 1986). Mixing acculturated clients with nonacculturated clients may lead to major discrepancies regarding the handling of a particular problem on the basis of differences in values or beliefs. For example, traditional values regarding dating, the role of the mother, or the impact of *machismo* shared by recent Hispanic immigrants may conflict with the view of more acculturated Hispanics. The Brief Acculturation Scale described in Chapter 2 may be helpful in screening Hispanic clients prior to placing these clients in a group therapy session.

A therapist involved in group therapy (and other forms of therapy) with Hispanic clients should master the pronunciation of Spanish names. As noted by Martinez (1986), when the therapist pronounces Spanish names correctly, this simple event may indicate to clients that the therapist is interested and concerned about their problems. One way to follow this guideline is to practice the Spanish names before the first group therapy session. The question, "How do you say your first and last name?" (*Cómo usted pronuncia su nombre y su apedillo*) is not recommended during the first group therapy session.

All members of the group should have the sense that the therapist will allow a great amount of flexibility, particularly in the areas of punctuality and attendance (Martinez, 1986). As noted by Sue and Sue (1990), the therapist should be aware that many Hispanic clients emphasize the "event" (e.g., social contacts with friends before attending a therapy session) rather than the "clock" (the assumption that clients should be on time or show up early for group therapy). This point should also be remembered during the programming of other interventions with Hispanic clients.

Behavioral Approaches

Behavioral approaches (e.g., behavior therapy, cognitive-behavior therapy, applied behavior analysis; Paniagua & Baer, 1981) are characterized by their emphasis on the experimental (empirical) analysis of the effect of interventions on behavioral changes and the assessment of these changes using reliable measures. These approaches, however, do not emphasize the potential impact of race and ethnicity during assessment and treatment. The overall assumption in these approaches is that the effectiveness of behavioral interventions is generalized across people regardless of race or ethnic background. Systematic desensitization and social-skills training are examples of empirically tested behavioral interventions recommended in the treatment of Hispanic clients (Jenkins & Ramsey, 1991). Despite empirical findings regarding the effectiveness of these techniques, if they are used with Hispanic clients, the following guidelines should be remembered.

The goal of systematic desensitization is to eliminate anxiety occurring in the presence of certain environmental events (Paniagua & Baer, 1981). The effectiveness of this treatment may be facilitated if the therapist uses Hispanic scenes (e.g., "Imagine that you are in a Mexican restaurant . . .") and a Spanish accent (Jenkins & Ramsey, 1991).

Teaching clients to be assertive by using appropriate social skills is the main goal of social-skills training (Lange & Jakubowski, 1976). In the absence of attention to cultural variables, this technique may be inappropriate, for example, in cases when the goal of intervention is to teach family members to deal with conflicts between an adolescent and parents, conflicts between husband and wife associated with the wife's intention to be assertive, and other situations in which the authority of the father or husband cannot be questioned. The value that Hispanics place on *respeto*, *machismo*, *marianismo*, and *familiarismo* are examples of major cultural variables that might discourage assertive behaviors in Hispanic males and females (Comas-Díaz & Duncan, 1985; Soto, 1983). For example, in many traditional Hispanic families, children and adolescents are not allowed to argue with their parents and respect toward the father is expected. In this case, teaching assertive behaviors to manage family conflicts involving an adolescent and his or her parents (e.g., saying to a Hispanic father "You don't want me to date Juan, but I will date him anyway") may be seen as a violation of a fundamental cultural values, namely, that properly respectful behavior toward the father is expected by all members of the family, including his children and his wife.

Similarly, a Hispanic female with a belief in *marianismo* and *machismo* would not feel comfortable (and might drop out from therapy) with a therapist interested in teaching her assertive behaviors toward her husband (e.g., "You should tell your husband what you think about him. You should be able to express your feelings openly"; or "Today, I will teach you how to reject orders from your husband"). Comas-Díaz and Duncan (1985) recommend teaching assertive behaviors with an emphasis upon a recognition of the authority of the father or husband before expressing assertive behaviors in a given context. For example, instead of teaching a woman how to reject orders from her husband, a better approach would be to teach her to use certain words that acknowledge the authority of the husband (e.g., "With all the respect that you deserve, I feel/believe . . ."). This statement places emphasis on *respeto* toward the husband, which is then followed by the expression of assertive behavior (". . . that I would prefer to visit my family this week"; Comas-Díaz & Duncan, 1985, p. 469).

Medication

Some therapists do not like to use medication for two reasons. First, they do not believe in the effect of drug therapy on the treatment of mental health problems. Second, if they do believe in the therapeutic effects of medication, therapists who are not physicians (e.g., psychologists, social workers) have to depend on the schedule and treatment regimen of a physician (e.g., a psychiatrist). In the treatment of Hispanic clients, however, a key guideline to remember is that many such clients expect medication for the treatment of their mental problems. This is particularly true in the case of Mexican Americans (Martinez, 1986). If medication is not mentioned during the process of psychotherapy, a Hispanic client may assume that the therapist is not a "good healer" and he or she may not come back for subsequent therapy.

If a Hispanic client expects medication for the treatment of his or her mental problem (keep in mind that some Hispanics may not want medication), the therapist should not forget that a large set of empirical data exists indicating that certain drugs may be effective in the management (not necessarily treatment) of certain mental problems, for example, the use of tricyclic antidepressants in the management of depression (Joyce & Paykel, 1989).

Regardless of disagreements with the use of medication (in terms of the above two reasons), recommending empirically tested drugs with clients who are expecting them during the therapy process may result in a placebo effect (i.e., the medication is not actually effective, but the client thinks that it is). If this works with a Hispanic client, the mental problem may become less severe over time and the therapist may claim that he or she was sensitive to the client's cultural expectation regarding the use of medication. A therapist treating Hispanic clients who does not wish to recommend medication may want to try it anyway.

If medication is used to manage mental disorders, five additional guidelines are suggested.

1. The therapist should ask the client directly about his or her expectancy for the prescription of medication to manage (or "cure" in the mind of the client) the problem.

2. If the therapist is not a medical doctor, he or she should be sure to consult with an adult or a child psychiatrist (they have more training and expertise in this area in comparison with general physicians) regarding the most appropriate medication for the target mental disorder.

3. The therapist should develop a checklist to screen the possibility of short-term and long-term side effects, and discuss these effects with the client each time he or she returns to the clinic. If side effects are reported by the client, they should be discussed with the person prescribing the medication.

4. The therapist should keep in mind that medication will not cure the mental disorder, but it might help in the management of the disorder.

5. The therapist should be aware of the tendency to rely exclusively on medication and ignore other aspects of therapy.

Music Therapy and Cuento Therapy

A Hispanic client may feel uncomfortable discussing a problem with the therapist. Music therapy may be recommended to assist the client in dealing indirectly with the main problem. The *plena* is recommended to communicate current events; *salsa* emphasizes struggle for survival; and the *bolero* states the nature of relationships. In the case of Hispanic children, *cuento therapy* (storytelling) is recommended with children who prefer to talk about their problems through readings by the therapist and interpretations of the readings by the child.

Avoid Insight-Oriented and Rational-Emotive Therapies

In general, insight-oriented psychotherapy emphasizes internal conflicts and blames the client for his or her own problems. Many Hispanics believe that problems emerge because of external conflicts with the environment and that other people should be blamed for one's own problems. Rational-emotive therapy is an argumentative and/or logistical talking therapy that competes with the cultural phenomenon of *machismo* shared by many Hispanic families.

5

Guidelines for the Assessment and Treatment of Asians

The third largest multicultural group in mental health services in the United States is Asian. In general, Asians comprise three major subgroups (Mollica, 1989; Mollica & Lavelle, 1988; Sue & Sue, 1990): Asian Americans (Japanese, Chinese, Filipinos, Asian Indians, and Koreans); Pacific Islanders (Hawaiians, Samoans, and Guamanians), and Southeast Asians (Vietnamese, Cambodians, and Laotians). In 1991, the Asian population in the United States (all three groups) was 7.023 million (U.S. Bureau of the Census, 1992).

Among Asians, the most numerous groups in the 1990 U.S. Census were Chinese (812,000), Filipinos (782,000), and Japanese (716,000; Kim et al., 1992). The majority of Asians live in urban areas, particularly in California, Texas, and Washington state. In 1991, the median income for Asians was $42,245, which was higher than both the national average ($35,262) and the average income level of whites ($36,915; U.S. Bureau of the Census, 1992). In 1980, 10.7% of Asian families lived below the poverty line (U.S. Bureau of the Census, 1983).

Among Asians, Southeast Asians are the most disadvantaged. For example, in summarizing the median income for Asians in 1980, Kim et al. (1992) report a median income for Vietnamese of $12,840, whereas the median income for Asian Americans and Pacific Islanders ranged from $20,459 to $27,657 and $14,242 to $19,196, respectively (in 1980, Japanese Americans had the higher median income, $27,354, and Samoans had the lower median income, $14,242). In 1980, the U.S. median income was $19,917. In addition, in 1980 35.1% of Vietnamese were below the poverty line, in comparison with much lower overall mean percentages below the poverty level as reported by Asian American subgroups (8.6%) and Pacific Islander subgroups (17.8%; Kim et al., 1992).

Cultural Variables That May
Affect Assessment and Treatment

Prejudice, Racism, and Discrimination

Prejudice, racism, and discrimination have historically been reported among Asians living in the United States (Sue and Sue, 1990; Yamamoto, 1986). This was particularly true during the immigration of Chinese who were brought in to work in the gold mines and railroads from the 1850s through World War II. The Chinese were followed by other Asians (Japanese, Filipinos, Koreans). Asian men who immigrated to this country as a resource for cheap labor during that period were considered "sneaky and sinister" and were prohibited from owning American land or bringing their wives with them. Discrimination was also apparent in housing employment and educational opportunities (Yamamoto, 1986). Yamamoto (1986) has noted that, despite significant improvement in the life of Asians in this country, "prejudice, racism, and discrimination still persist" against this group (p. 92). Thus non-Asian therapists should be sensitive to the historical events among Asians in the United States and should avoid verbal and nonverbal behaviors that could be interpreted by Asian clients as signs of prejudice, racism, or discrimination.

Familism

Asians place great emphasis upon the individual-family relationship (Ho, 1992; Sue & Sue, 1990): The family is paramount. American individualism is not rewarded and, like Hispanics, Asians view individualism as an example of the individual's peculiarities. Like Hispanic and African American families, Asians also place great emphasis upon the extended family. Among Asians, however, the role for each family member must be very clear and cannot be changed. Like Hispanic families, the role of the father is to function as the dominant figure in the family; his authority is preeminent. The sense of role flexibility generally seen among African Americans is not emphasized among Asian Americans.

Role of Children and Wife

Among traditional Asians, the primary duty of children is to be good and to respect their parents. Parents can determine children's personal desires and ambitious, and any attempt not to comply with parents' expectations is seen as a threat toward the parents' authority. Asian women are expected to marry, be obedient, act as helpers, have children, and respect the authority of their father. This may explain why Asian women and children appear less autonomous and assertive and more conforming, dependent, inhibited, and obedient to authority than Anglo women and children (Ho, 1992; Sue & Sue, 1990). These are appropriate (or normal) behavior patterns among Asians. A therapist who considers the independence of an individual from his or her family as an example of autonomy and assertiveness in that individual would interpret these behavior patterns among Asians as inappropriate. However, a therapist familiar with Asian behavior patterns would avoid emphasizing the independence of children and adolescents from the authority of their parents in an Asian family. Such a therapist would also avoid a discussion regarding the lack of assertive behaviors and autonomy in Asian women during the process of family therapy.

Public Suppression of Problems

In general, Asians do not encourage members of the group to express their problems to people outside the group (Sue & Sue, 1990). All problems (including physical and mental problems) must be shared only among family members, just as all credits and successes received by an individual must also be shared by the entire family. Emphasis on shame and guilt are mechanisms used by Asian families to enforce norms in the family (Dana, 1993a). These mechanisms play a crucial role in preventing Asians from reporting or admitting their problems in public.

If an Asian person does not show the behaviors expected within and outside the family, he or she may lose confidence and support from the family, which could lead to the development of a strong sense of shame and guilt. This sense of shame and guilt may lead to considerable anxiety and depression. Several Asian scholars (Ho, 1992; Sue & Sue, 1990) note that this sense of shame and guilt may explain the strong self-control and self-discipline often reported among Asians. Thus an important guideline is for the therapist to explore this sense of shame and guilt to understand how difficult it is for Asian clients to talk about their problems in public.

Because of this normative and cultural approach to shame and guilt, a therapist should not expect that an Asian client will report his or her emotional problems as soon as the request "Tell me about your problems" is made. (Many African American and Hispanic clients tend to respond to this question the first time they interact with the therapist.)

Indirect Versus Direct
Forms of Communication

When Asians are exposed to verbal communication, they often look quiet, act passive, make a great deal of effort to avoid offending others, sometimes answer all questions affirmatively to be polite when they cannot understand the therapist's questions, and avoid eye contact (Chung, 1992; Root, Ho, & Sue, 1986). This indirect form of verbal communication is very appropriate among Asians. This communication pattern differs from the direct form of verbal communication based on western standards of communication in which both the speaker (e.g., the client) and the listener (e.g., the therapist) must look expressive, be active, and generally not answer questions that cannot be understood.

Silence and lack of eye contact are forms of indirect communication that may create problems during the assessment and treatment of Asian clients. Among Asians, silence is a sign of respect, politeness, and a desire to continue speaking after making a point during a conversation (Sue & Sue, 1990).

Eye contact during direct verbal communication is expected in western culture because it implies attention and respect toward others. Among Asians, however, eye contact is considered a sign of lack of respect and attention, particularly to authority (e.g., parents) and older people. A therapist who does not understand the use of silence and lack of eye contact by Asians may feel uncomfortable and may change the content of the conversation on the assumption that the client is not interested in a particular point or is not attending to what the therapist is saying. This tactic may prevent Asian clients from elaborating on a prior point or demonstrating an acceptable way of attention and respect toward the listener.

The First Session

Exhibit Expertise and Authority

Many Asian clients come to their first therapy session believing that the therapist will tell them what is wrong and how to resolve their problems (Sue & Sue, 1990). In addition, in the mind of many Asian clients the therapist is the authority. The therapist, then, must demonstrate these two qualities (expertise and authority) during the first session to ensure that the client will return to the clinic. Kim (1985) suggests the following practical guidelines to assist Asian clients in recognizing the expertise and authority of the therapist during the first session.

1. Casually mention prior experiences with other clients with similar problems. For example, the therapist could say "In my experience with many similar cases . . ." (to show expertise), or "In my professional judgment . . ." (to show authority).
2. Display diplomas, licenses, books.
3. Use a professional title when making introductions (e.g., "I am Doctor . . ." or "I am Professor . . .").
4. Provide possible reasons or explanations for the cause of the problem.
5. Give the impression that a tentative solution (cure) to the problem is possible.
6. Emphasize concrete and tangible goals and avoid comments suggesting that the therapy will take a long period of time (for Asian clients, only inexperienced doctors need a lot of time to understand and resolve a problem).

Maintain Formality and Conversational Distance

In general, Asians tend to perceive the therapist as the authority; they feel that their role is to be passive, respectful, and obedient in the presence of the therapist (Yamamoto, 1986). Thus *formalism* in the therapist-client relationship is expected among Asian clients. The initial contact between the therapist and an Asian client is generally formal; the client will not be overly friendly during the first meeting. Jokes should be avoided during this session. The nature of the relationship often determines the *conversation distance* between Asians and other people. The therapist should allow the client to define that distance during the process of assessment and treatment. For example, the therapist should sit first and allow the Asian client to determine the conversation distance. If a trusting relationship between the Asian client and the therapist is not yet built, the client will not sit close to the therapist (Chung, 1992).

Do Not Expect an Open/Public
Discussion of Emotional Problems

An individual's emotional problems bring shame and guilt to the Asian family, preventing any family member from reporting such problems to others outside the family. This phenomenon probably explains why the prevalence of emotional disorders among Asian clients seems very low in current epidemiological data involving mental disorders across multicultural groups (Sue & Sue, 1990). In the first session with an Asian client, the therapist must show both verbally and nonverbally that he or she will wait until the client is ready to discuss mental problems in public. This waiting period may include more than one session, and the Asian client should sense this possibility.

Expect Expression of Mental
Problems in Somatic Terms

Asians tend to express psychological disorders in somatic terms (Ho, 1992; Hughes, 1993; Sue & Sue, 1990). This phenomenon is associated with the shame, humiliation, and guilt that could result from making these problems public (Hughes, 1993). Given the choice to an Asian client of talking about physical symptoms (e.g., chest pains, headaches, and fatigue) or talking about psychiatric symptoms (e.g., hallucinations, delusions), an Asian client would probably select the first choice, because reports of physical complaints are often more acceptable (i.e., result in less shame, humiliation, and guilt) than reports about emotional or psychiatric problems in Asian communities (Sue & Sue, 1990).

Thus, when an Asian client consults with a therapist for the first time, he or she may spend a great deal of time talking about physical (medical) complications such as headaches, back pain, weight loss, and fatigue. Two guidelines are recommended (Ho, 1992; Sue & Sue, 1990) to handle Asian clients' somatization of psychological or psychiatric disorders during the first session. First, the therapist should always acknowledge these somatic complaints. He or she should also tell the client that medical consultations (particularly with an Asian physician) for the clinical assessment of potential physical disorders will be arranged before the therapist concludes that the client is exhibiting some form of somatization disorder (e.g., conversion disorder, hypochondriasis, somatoform pain disorder) rather than a true physical disorder. Second, the therapist should introduce statements that allow the client to move from verbalizations of somatic complaints to verbalizations involving mental health problems gradually. For example, the therapist could say, "I will consult with a physician for your headaches. Perhaps you are having headaches because you do not know what to do to handle some conflicts in your life. Would you like to talk about these conflicts?" The therapist should avoid statements that indicate that he or she does not believe that the client "really" has a physical (medical) problem. The statement "You don't have headaches. You simply want to avoid talking about your mental problems" is not recommended.

Consider the First Session a Crisis

Because many Asian families believe that mental illness can bring shame and humiliation to the entire family, these families often refuse to seek professional mental help and tend to wait for many years (5 to 10 years) before seeking such help (Fujii, Fukushima, & Yamamoto, 1993; Gaw, 1993b). Thus, when the client is brought to the attention of a clinician, family members are often in a state of crisis because of their inability to handle a chronic and severe condition that has developed over time. For this reason, the first meeting with Asian clients should always be considered a potential crisis. Because of this possibility of crisis or emergency, the clinician should be prepared to display two emergency responses:

1. Immediate assessment of suicide attempts and thoughts
2. Immediate attention to the presenting problem and its treatment (including the availability of family supports, possibility of brief inpatient treatment, and consultation with social agencies involved with Asian communities)

In the second case, the therapist should inform the family whether the client needs brief psychotherapy, inpatient treatment, and/or medication before the termination of the first session. Yamamoto (1986) points out that these guidelines are particularly important with elderly Asians referred to outpatient mental health clinics because of the high frequency of suicidal behavior among elderly Asians living in the United States (approximately 27 in 100,000); the occurrence of this behavior is extremely low among elderly Asians living in their countries of origin.

Avoid Discussing Hospitalization

Although it is appropriate to consider the first meeting with an Asian client as a potential crisis situation, it is also important to avoid comments regarding the hospitalization of the client during the first meeting. Many Asians consider hospitalization as the last resort and expect to hear about alternatives to psychiatric hospitalization (e.g., outpatient treatment and the delivery of treatments by family members at home) during the first meeting. If hospitalization of an Asian client is necessary during the first meeting (e.g., because the client is a danger to himself, herself, or others), the following guidelines should be followed (Fujii et al., 1993; Kinzie & Leung, 1993).

1. Family members must be consulted and must approve the hospitalization.
2. Family members and the client must receive a detailed description of the length of stay, recommended tests, and treatment modality.
3. Family members should be told about visiting hours and the reason why having a family member in the hospital with the client is not encouraged (e.g., for clinical or administrative reasons).
4. Family members should be told that they may bring their inpatient relative ethnic foods to replace or supplement western-style foods offered in the hospital.
5. During the entire period of hospitalization, the client should never be told about his or her diagnosis. Only the family and the therapist should share this information. Many Asians believe that if the patient knows "the truth about an illness, he or she might lose hope and deteriorate more quickly" (Fujii et al., 1993, p. 337).

Consider Alternative Care Services

It is a good tactic with Asian clients to assume that the present problem is a chronic problem developed over a long period. Despite the severity of the clinical case, however, many Asian families may not agree with the need to hospitalize their relatives. Therefore, prior to actual contact with an Asian client, the therapist should determine the availability of alternative care services. For example, instead of hospitalization, it would be more acceptable by an Asian family to consider the care of the client at home with some professional assistance. A listing of mental health community services for Asians should also be available during the first session (examples of such services are listed below). These alternatives could facilitate the assessment and treatment of Asian families who refuse the hospitalization of a relative to avoid the resulting stigma of mental illness (Yamamoto, 1986, p. 117).

Examples of Alternative Services for Asian Clients

- Asian Community Service Center in Los Angeles
- Pacific/Asian Preventive Program in San Diego

- Richmond Area Multi-Service Center in San Francisco
- Asian Counseling and Referral Service in Seattle
- Asian American Drug Abuse Program in Los Angeles
- Center for Southeast Asian Refugee Resettlement in San Francisco
- Asian Counseling and Treatment Center in Los Angeles
- Korean American Mental Health Service Center in Los Angeles
- Operation Samahan in San Diego (specializes in outpatient health care for Filipino clients)

Provide Concrete and Tangible Advice

Asian clients want the therapist to deal with their immediate concerns by providing concrete and tangible advice (Root et al., 1986; Sue & Sue, 1990). Prolonged verbal exchanges between the client and the therapist should be avoided. Suggestions that appear ambiguous should also be avoided. For example, the statement "Mr. Sue, you need to change your behavior in a positive way if you want your wife to stay with you" tells nothing about exactly what Mr. Sue should do.

In addition, solutions to problems involving long-range goals should not be discussed during the first session. For example, the following statement is both ambiguous and implies a long-term goal: "Let's talk about what you need to do to change your behavior in the next 6 months. What do you think you should do to improve your relationship with your wife?" A better statement with an Asian client would be "During the next 5 days, write on a piece of paper the number of times you and your wife hold hands, eat, and take short walks together. When you return for therapy next week, we will talk about what you wrote." This statement is concrete (i.e., it tells the client exactly what to do to improve the relationship), and it suggests a short-term goal (i.e., the task assigned to the client will be discussed the following week).

Psychotherapy Is Not Expected

During the first session, Asian clients expect that the therapist wants to know about the client in general. Conducting psychotherapy to deal with the client's problem is not expected during the first session (and in some cases several sessions may be necessary before psychotherapy can be initiated). As noted above, if the therapist determines that he or she is dealing with an emergency situation or crisis, the use of inpatient treatment and/or medication should be considered.

In general, however, an Asian client will not expect the use of psycho-therapy (or other forms of intervention) during the first session. Because the public admission of problems (particularly mental problems) is not encouraged among Asians, the therapist cannot expect the Asian client to share his or her feelings and emotional problems with someone outside his or her immediate family during the first session (Sue & Sue, 1990). The best approach is to give a sense that the therapist is available to listen and understands that the client may not agree to discuss emotional problems openly for several sessions.

Consider the Client's Organic Explanation of Emotional Problems

Because Asian clients tend to express their emotional problems in somatic terms (Sue & Sue, 1990), these clients generally place a great deal of emphasis on the explanation of their emotional problems in terms of organic variables. For this reason, most Asian clients expect medication (to deal with these organic problems) during their first contact with a therapist. A practical guideline in this case is to accept the client's own interpretation of the origin of his or her mental problems as an example of the client's belief system. This tactic could greatly enhance the therapist-client relationship in future sessions. If medication will not be recom-mended during the first session, the therapist should discuss the reason for not prescribing medication in concrete terms. The statement "I don't think you need medication" is ambiguous because the client needs to know why medication will not be prescribed. A better statement would be "To improve communication between you and your wife, I would like to recommend a technique based on learning how to solve problems. Medi-cation is an alternative that I might consider later, after consulting with your physician regarding the medication you are currently taking to pre-vent complications by combining two or more medications."

Do Not Try to Know Everything During the Meeting

In general, practitioners are trained to conduct a thorough clinical interview (meaning getting as much information as possible during that meeting) during the first meeting with a client. This approach is not recommended with Asian clients (Gaw, 1993b). Questions dealing with specific and sensitive issues (e.g., "How is your sexual relationship with your wife?") should be avoided, and more general statements are sug-

gested (e.g., "How is the relationship between you and your wife?").
Emphasis upon general statements could enhance the therapist-client therapeutic relationship and prepare the way for questioning the client about
intimate matters in subsequent sessions.

Southeast Asian Clients

The above guidelines are suggested with all Asian clients. The following
guidelines are strongly recommended specifically with Southeast Asian
clients (Cook & Timberlake, 1989; Mollica, 1989; Mollica & Lavelle,
1988; Sue & Sue, 1990). As noted above, many Southeast Asian clients
come to the United States with a history of traumatic events generally not
reported by other Asians (particularly Asian Americans or Pacific Islanders). For this reason, the first session with a Southeast Asian client should
be planned carefully. Below are examples of specific points to consider
with this group when that session is planned (Ho, 1992; Mollica & Lavelle,
1988; Sue & Sue, 1990).

Avoid Questions Dealing
With Traumatic Events

During the first session with this group, it is extremely important to
avoid statements, questions, or commentaries dealing with traumatic events.
The therapist must be familiar with the fact that many of these clients come
to therapy with a history of torture, killing of loved ones, missing family
members, witnessed killing, and sexual abuse acts. It would be extremely
difficult for the patient to discuss these events openly during his or her
first meeting with the therapist. Because of the long history of traumatic
events among Southeast Asians, such a client should not leave the clinic
without an assessment of suicide attempts, organic brain syndrome (because of potential head injury), and depression.

Do Not Encourage the Client to Say
More Than What He or She Wants To

Encouraging a Southeast Asian to talk about his or her problems during
the first session could be very stressful for the client. Thus these clients
should not be encouraged to say more than what they are actually saying
at the present moment. For example, the statements "Are you sure that this
is the reason why you need help?" or "Do you think that some dreams about

very bad events in your life are creating problems?" should always be avoided during the first session.

Provide a Sense That Stress
Will Be Reduced as Quickly as Possible

Southeast Asian clients expect help from the therapist in terms of providing quick solutions for their level of stress, often caused by a lack of resources for housing, food, clothing, and other vital elements for their survival in the United States (Cook & Timberlake, 1989). In this case, the therapist should be familiar with social services (particularly agencies specifically created to deal with refugees) in the community that could assist the client with his or her needs to minimize the level of stress.

Conducting Psychotherapy

The following guidelines, recommended when conducting psychotherapy with Asians, are selected from Chung (1992), Ho (1992), Mollica and Lavelle (1988), Murase (1992), Root et al. (1986), Sue and Sue (1990), and Yamamoto (1986).

Educate Asian Clients

Because many Asian clients do not understand terms such as therapy, psychotherapy, verbal therapy, psychodynamic therapy, and behavior therapy and how these therapies differ from traditional (healing) methods, the therapist should begin the psychotherapy process with a brief discussion of the meaning of such terms (Kim, 1993).

Conduct an Assessment of
Shame and Humiliation

During psychotherapy with Asian clients, the therapist should conduct an assessment of the persistence of shame and humiliation resulting from the stigma of mental illness and discuss this issue with the client and family members. After the first meeting (which is often a crisis situation), an assessment of the persistence of shame and humiliation could include attention to the following points (Gaw, 1993b).

1. The client or a family member is extremely concerned about the qualifications of the therapist.
2. The client is excessively worried about confidentiality.
3. The client refuses to cover expenses with private insurance.
4. The client has difficulty keeping appointments, or frequently arrives late for therapy.
5. Family members refuse to support the treatment.
6. The client insists on receiving services from an Anglo clinician, to avoid Asian therapists.
7. The client refuses to seek treatment even if a severe mental health problem is evident.

The therapist may use this assessment to infer that the client is having problems talking openly about mental problems because of the shame and humiliation resulting from the public admission of such problems.

Discuss the Duration of Therapy

Most Asians expect a quick solution to their mental problems. As noted above, Asians often seek professional services for chronic psychiatric disorders. Asian clients should be informed that a quick solution of chronic mental health problems is unrealistic, and they should be informed about the approximate duration of treatment (Yamamoto et al., 1993). Long-term treatment periods with emphasis on uncovering underlying conflicts are not recommended with Asian clients (Murase, 1992). Short-term treatment periods, no longer than 2 or 3 months, are recommended. An extension of these short-term treatment periods must be negotiated with the client.

Avoid Personalism

In comparison with Hispanics, Asian clients do not expect personalism during psychotherapy; the formal relationship established in the first session is expected to continue in subsequent sessions.

Recommended Modalities of Therapies

Medication

Medication is expected by many Asian clients. However, drug dosages recommended for Anglos cannot automatically be prescribed for Asian clients because of "differences in body weight and possible ethnic differences in drug metabolism and sensitivities" (Gaw, 1993, p. 276). If medication is used with Asians, the recommendation is to use low doses because of the tendency of these clients to respond at much lower doses in comparison with non-Asian clients (Fujii et al., 1993; Kinzie & Leung, 1993). Because many Asian clients use herbal medications to treat physical and mental problems, the therapist should discuss potential side effects resulting from the consumption of traditional medicines in combination with psychotropic medication.

Behavioral Approaches

Behavioral approaches (e.g., behavior therapy techniques) are recommended with Asian clients because these approaches are concrete and directive and do not emphasize the exploration of internal conflicts leading to enhancement of the shame that the client experiences by reporting his or her problems.

Family Therapy

Family therapy with Asian clients is recommended for two reasons (Berg & Jaya, 1993). First, among Asians the family (as a unit) is more important than the individual. Second, the word "privacy" (in the sense of withholding information from family members) is foreign to many Asians (Hughes, 1993; Sue & Sue, 1990). Thus an Asian client would expect his or her family to be actively involved in his or her assessment and treatment and the therapist would be expected to share information regarding assessment and treatment issues with all family members (not only with the client). Additional guidelines in the programming of family therapy with Asian clients include the following (Berg & Jaya, 1993):

1. Problem-solving techniques used to deal with marital problems and conflict between children and parents should emphasize a process of negotiation rather than a process of head-on confrontation. In this process of negotiation, the therapist is seen as the mediator, who is expected to be an expert in a position of authority.

2. To enhance a peaceful negotiation, the client or the parties in conflict should be seen separately before family members are seen together in family therapy sessions.

3. The differences in age and status should be considered when the therapist addresses family members. For example, the head of the family should always be addressed first using his or her last name and any title

(e.g., Mr. Sue, Dr. Sue, Mrs. Sue). During the therapy process, an Asian client may ask the therapist to call him or her by first name; until this request is evident, the therapist should maintain a formal relationship with the client. As noted by Berg and Jaya (1993), many Asian clients believe that the respect they receive from a therapist is more important than what the therapist does to help them to solve their problems.

4. Family therapy must be problem focused, goal oriented, and symptom relieving on a short-term basis (Kim, 1985). Emphasis on internal conflicts, self-assertion, expression of anger, and acquisition of insights as goals in family therapy is not recommended with Asian clients (Kim, 1985). Such clients would expect a therapist to define the goals of family therapy in terms of situational changes requiring external solutions.

5. Because of the expected parental authoritative role by children toward their parents (Ho, 1993), the programming of family therapy leading to the development of the independence of Asian children and adolescents from their parents is not recommended. In their social contacts with American children, however, Asian children quickly learn that in the typical American parenting style democracy is emphasized in which children are allowed to speak and question authority, and encouraged to be independent. The sharing of power among family members in the western culture may compete with the vertical, hierarchical structure of Asian families in which parents (particularly the father) are in a position of unquestionable authority (Kim, 1985). Thus, before scheduling family therapy with an Asian family, the therapist must determine whether all family members in therapy share the same value concerning the expected undisputable leadership and authority of parents. In this process, an evaluation of the level of acculturation among family members is recommended (see discussion on acculturation in Chapters 2 and 8).

6. Because Asians emphasize the family first (and the individual second), relationship questions are recommended during the process of assessment and treatment (Berg & Jaya, 1993). For example, the following questions do not emphasize a relationship between the client and other family members: "What do you think about your problem?" "If you stop drinking after treatment, how will you feel?" "How does this problem affect you?" The same questions can be phrased in terms of a relationship between the client and other family members. For example, "What do you think your father will say is the main problem between you and him?" "If you stop drinking after treatment, what will your family notice you doing differently?" "How does this problem affect your family?"

7. The therapist should always avoid embarrassing family members in front of each other and in front of the therapist. The therapist should always

protect the dignity and self-respect of the client and his or her family. This guideline is often termed "saving face" (Berg & Jaya, 1993; Kim, 1993). For example, an Asian father would "lose face" during family therapy if he is told by the therapist (in the presence of other family members) that he is "wrong" in demanding that the son cannot select a profession that is unacceptable to his parents. To avoid embarrassing the father in the presence of his son, the therapist should compliment the father and reframe the issue in a positive way. For example, "I understand that you would like your son to have a profession that could help the family's financial situation. But would you agree that your son would be happier if he selects a profession that is rewarding to him and to the family?" In this case, the therapist would preserve the dignity and proper role of the father and provide an alternative solution to the problem (i.e., allowing the son and his parents to make a compromise regarding the selection of the son's profession).

8. If the central issue in family therapy is divorce, the following practical guidelines are recommended (Ho, 1993). First, because divorce is not socially acceptable among Asian communities and is seen as a very important decision by family members, the practitioner should not provide the idea of divorce as an alternative and should wait until the client clearly indicates that it is time to discuss this alternative. Second, many Asian clients are not familiar with legal divorce proceedings; the practitioner should provide the client with legal information and the names, addresses, and phone numbers of lawyers with knowledge of and expertise in the client's cultural background. Third, relatives and close friends may feel that the client's decision to divorce could bring shame to the entire family, which may lead to the withdrawal of social and economic supports. The practitioner should assist the client in finding new support systems by encouraging the client to meet other Asian divorcees who share the same experiences. This third guideline may be implemented through the scheduling of group therapy involving clients sharing similar experiences.

9. The assumption is that Asian clients prefer to involve the entire family in the assessment and treatment of their mental disorders. However, this assumption must be carefully evaluated with each client. As noted by Yamamoto (1986), acculturated Asian clients may or may not want family members involved in psychotherapy. Thus, despite the assumption that family ties are paramount among many Asians, the therapist should avoid a recommendation of family therapy on the basis of only this assumption. A careful assessment of acculturation is recommended (see Table 8.1 for examples of acculturation scales recommended for Asians).

Avoid Talking Therapy

Talking therapy is not recommended with Asian clients. For many Asian clients, active therapy (i.e., doing something to deal with the problem quickly) has more value than a "talking cure" (Gaw, 1993b, p. 276). As noted by Tsui (1985), Asian clients "expect tangible evidence of intervention, not abstract discussion" (p. 360). For this reason, therapies based on self-exploration and psychodynamic interpretations of symptoms are considered ineffective with Asian clients.

Select Group Therapy Carefully

Because of their tendency to avoid sharing their problems with people outside the immediate family, Asian clients are not good candidates for group therapy. This guideline is particularly relevant with sensitive issues such as sexual dysfunction and infertility (Tsui, 1985). However, group therapy would be appropriate in cases when the client's support system (relatives and close friends) is not available and an alternative support system is quickly needed. For example, Asian clients who elect to divorce and do not receive support from their relatives and close friends could share their experiences with other Asian clients who also were neglected by their family and friends because of a similar "misbehavior" (see Ho, 1987, p. 63).

Additional Guidelines for
Southeast Asian Clients

In addition to the above guidelines recommended for all Asian clients, three specific guidelines are suggested during the process of psychotherapy with Southeast Asian clients.

First, despite the role of the extended family, a discussion of the potential use of family therapy should be considered carefully because the family may not be available (e.g., due to deaths in the family during war).

Second, the therapist should assist the client in the pursuit of three categories of services (Flaskerud & Anh, 1988). For community and education services, the therapist should provide information to the client regarding mental health centers as resources for treatment, education about mental disorders, and education about American society (including culture and lifestyle). For social services, the client should be informed about financial assistance, community resources for food and housing, and vocational and language training opportunities in the community. The client should also be informed about culturally relevant assessment and treatment for mental disorders, family-related problems, and adjustment problems.

Third, recent reports indicate that approximately 50% of Southeast Asian refugees in the general population could be suffering from posttraumatic stress disorder (PTSD; Kinzie & Leung, 1993). Therefore, after the first contact with a Southeast Asian refugee, the therapist should screen for PTSD during the psychotherapy process and discuss specific stressful events responsible for this disorder. The therapist, however, should keep in mind that Southeast Asian clients may not discuss feelings involving traumatic experiences either because these clients do not wish to reveal severe traumas voluntarily during the initial evaluation, or the primary symptoms for PTSD (e.g., recurrent distressing dreams, irritability) are not generally mentioned by these clients because they think these symptoms are unrelated to the presenting problem, or because many refugees simply avoid talking about traumatic events under any situation. In addition, a Southeast Asian refugee might not talk about these events because he or she realizes that the clinician does not want to listen "to the terrible stories and the agony endured by the refugees" (Kinzie & Leung, 1993, p. 290).

Social-Skills Training

Social-skills training is particularly recommended with Asian refugee immigrants with severe fear of deportation or fear that they may give a bad reputation to other Asians because of their assertive behaviors (Yamamoto et al., 1993).

6

=========

Guidelines for the Assessment and Treatment of American Indians

The American Indian population is the fourth major multicultural group in mental health services in the United States (Thompson, Walker, & Silk-Walker, 1993). The American Indian population is also known as Native Americans, but this term is not recommended because it does not include other Indian groups in the United States (e.g., Eskimos, Aleuts) and Indians from other countries (e.g., Canadian and Mexican Indians) who have settled in the United States (Fleming, 1992). The preferred terms are American Indian and Alaska Native (Fleming, 1992; Thompson et al., 1993). Thompson et al. (1993) suggest that the term Indian should be used to "refer to all American Indian, Alaska Natives, and Canadian and Mexican Indian people" (p. 189).

In terms of the assessment and treatment of Indians in the continental United States, American Indians constitute the most common group seen in mental health services (Ho, 1992; Richardson, 1981). In addition, historical analyses involving the precontact period (i.e., the time before the North American continent was "discovered" by Europeans in 1492) and subsequent periods emphasize American Indians (Walker & LaDue, 1986). The majority of historical and clinical materials reported in this chapter are representative of American Indians.

In 1991, the American Indian (all groups) population was 1.9 (U.S. Bureau of the Census, 1992). The majority of American Indians presently live in six states: Alaska, Arizona, California, Oklahoma, New Mexico, and Washington (U.S. Bureau of the Census, 1992). Approximately 339,836 American Indians live on 278 federal and state reservations; most reservations have fewer than 1,000 Indians (Ho, 1992). In 1980, the median income for American Indians was $13,724 (U.S. Bureau of the Census, 1983). Estimates for American Indians living in reservations is much lower (approximately $9,942; Ho, 1992). In 1980, 23.7% of American Indians were living below the poverty level, in comparison with 9.6% of the U.S. population (Kim et al., 1992). Among the four groups discussed in this text, American Indians are generally the most disadvantaged in terms of socioeconomic characteristics, mortality, and life expectancy (Kim et al., 1992; U.S. Department of Human Services, 1991).

Is the Client an Authentic Indian?

If an American Indian wants to be considered for assistance from federal Indian programs, he or she must prove the status of being an Indian in terms of the definition established by the federal government (Ho, 1992; Sue & Sue, 1990; Trimble & Fleming, 1989; Wise & Miller, 1983). This definition states that the client must have at least one-quarter Indian "blood" and a proof of tribal status (Harjo, 1993; Ho, 1993). However, the federal government does not have the final word in that definition; the federal government must recognize the sovereign status of each tribal definition of "Indian" (McDonald, 1994; O'Brien, 1989). Because it is extremely difficult to apply this definition in clinical practices, practitioners should seek consultation from Indian organizations (see Table 6.1) and tribal leaders in cases when the assistance of federal programs is necessary to manage the case but the client is not sure of his or her Indian status at the moment of contact with the mental health agency. The worse approach would be to ask the client, "Are you sure that you meet the definition of an Indian in this country?"

Cultural Variables That May
Affect Assessment and Treatment

Historical Events and Their
Impact on Mental Health Services

Walker and LaDue (1986) suggest that practitioners who want to assess and treat American Indians should be familiar with critical events occur-

Table 6.1 Organizations for American Indians

Association on American Indian Affairs
432 Park Avenue South
New York, NY 10016
212-689-8720

Dull Knife Memorial College
P. O. Box 98
Lame Deer, MT 39040
406-477-6219

National Indian Social Worker's Association
1740 West 41st Street
Tulsa, OK 74107
505-446-8432

Northwest Indian Child Welfare Association
Box 751
Portland, OR 97207
503-725-3038

The Indian Family Circle Project
New Mexico Department of Social Services
P.O. Box Drawer 5160
Santa Fe, NM 87502
505-827-8400

Urban Indian Child Resource Center
390 Euclid Avenue
Oakland, CA 94610
510-356-2121

---

ring during four time intervals and the impact of these events among American Indian clients: the precontact period, prior to 1492; the Manifest Destiny period, 1492-1890; the assimilation period, 1890-1970; and the self-determination period, 1970 to the present.

Precontact Period

Many of American Indians' rules, roles, values, and beliefs were developed during the precontact period. An important element in that period is the "survival pact," which included the rules that govern the "symbiotic relationship among the individual, the group, and the earth. . . . [These rules] touched all aspects of life, including marriage and social encounters, food gathering, hunting and fishing, religion, and medicine. . . . As long as tribes followed these rules, they survived and prospered" (Walker & LaDue, 1986, p. 145). These features of the survival pact have passed from generation to generation by way of legends, stories, and songs.

A recent example of what might happen to the individual or the group if the survival pact is violated is the mystery illness (a flulike illness that provoked acute respiratory distress and deaths) experienced by the Navajo Nation in 1993 and the explanation of the origin of this illness by many Navajos. According to reports published in the *Houston Chronicle*, a Navajo reported that "the tribal elders . . . feel that the disease is a prophecy of Mother Earth right . . . The medicine men are saying [the illness occurred] because of something we have done wrong, for not taking better care of the Earth" (Foreman, 1993, p. 18A). Health officials from New Mexico reported that the mystery illness was caused by the Hanta virus, which is present in rodent droppings and urine. On the basis of this information, western doctors consulted with the medicine men in an effort to minimize fears and deal with the disease. This example not only illustrates the function of the survival pact among American Indians (exemplified by America's largest Indian tribe, the Navajo Nation), but it also shows the role that medicine men play today in a crisis and the attention and respect they receive from the scientific community.

Manifest Destiny

Two important events during this period (1492-1890) were the impact of epidemics upon the lives of many Indian people and the development of racism and discrimination with the creation of reservations and boarding schools. A familiarity with both events will help practitioners understand why many American Indian clients do not trust Anglo mental health professionals.

Diseases such as smallpox, cholera, malaria, pneumonia, syphilis, diphtheria, and typhoid fever are generally considered examples of European diseases that early explorers (white men from other lands) introduced to American Indians (Brandon, 1989; Walker & LaDue, 1986). These diseases produced massive numbers of deaths among Indians. A consequence of the devastating effect of such epidemics was a drastic change in many of the features of the survival pact. For example, prior to the epidemics, the job of the medicine man was to cure all diseases regardless of their causes. European diseases, however, were not examples of diseases the medicine man was able to cure. Thus the medicine man was "of little practical or spiritual value to his tribe" (Walker & LaDue, 1986, p. 153). In addition, the epidemics killed many of the elders and tribal leaders who taught the rules of the survival pact (e.g., the harmony between the group and the earth as a measure of stability in the tribe, beliefs in supernatural and spiritual events, values and rules of behavior). This led to the loss of the meaning of the survival pact, which prior to the epidemics, was considered a critical element in the mind of many American Indians.

The European diseases not only contributed to the loss of many features of the survival pact, but it also led to the conversion to Christianity. Walker and LaDue (1986) suggest that this conversion occurred for two reasons. First, the epidemics left little hope among the Indians for a "return to the traditional ways" (p. 156). Second, "the Christian promise of a better afterlife must have seemed quite inviting" (p. 156). It is now clear that the role of Christianity during such epidemics was to impose Christian beliefs and rules of conduct on the tribes, including the elimination of cultural value of the survival pact.

The creation of the reservations was initially considered by American Indians as a positive event in their struggle to move away from the influence of whites on their lives, culture, language, and religion (Walker & LaDue, 1986). Thus tribes were relocated in areas called reservations remote from white settlement. American Indians were promised vast amounts of lands and protection from the influences of whites. These promises were broken many times: Lands were reduced; tribes were relocated; existing reservations were eliminated; legislation was introduced making the language, religion, and customs of Indians illegal; and tribal leaders were exiled. These events "make reservations unhappy and miserable" (Walker & LaDue, 1986, p. 157).

Another negative event was the creation of the boarding schools by the government and various (non-Indian) religious groups (Reyhner & Eder, 1988). The main goal of these schools was to replace the practice of Indian language, dress, beliefs, religion, and customs with the practice of the white civilization. In such schools, Indian "children were punished severely for speaking their own language . . . [and the message was that] to be Indian was to be bad" (Walker & LaDue, 1986, p. 157).

Assimilation

This period (1890-1970) reinforced the development of racism and discrimination experienced by American Indians during the creation of the reservations and boarding schools (O'Brien, 1989). During the early years of the assimilation period, Indians had two choices: death or the assimilation of the white culture. Many Indians moved away from their old traditions, not only to avoid death but as a result of the deaths of the great chiefs, who were instrumental in the transmission of such traditions to their people (Walker & LaDue, 1986).

Despite these negative events, old traditions among tribes continued during the assimilation period and two important victories occurred in the lives of American Indians: Indians became the last people in this country to receive full citizenship and voting privileges, and the Indian Reorganization Act was passed that, among other things, gave American Indians the right to govern their people using traditional values and their own culture (O'Brien, 1989). These victories, however, were followed in the 1950s by another attempt from whites to force Indians to assimilate the standards of the white society. These attempts are called *termination* and *relocation* (Walker & LaDue, 1986). Termination involved the elimination of all special agreements and relationships between the federal government and tribes. Relocation consisted of moving American Indians living on reservations into urban cities. These measures led to increases in already existing social (e.g., cultural ambivalence) and behavior (e.g., depression, alcoholism) problems among Indians, but whites again failed to eliminate the Indian culture and old values.

Self-Determination

This period (1970 to the present) has been characterized by an increase in the number of Indians in leadership roles in federal Indian programs and four congressional acts to benefit Indians (Goodluck, 1993; O'Brien, 1989; Walker & LaDue, 1986): the Indian Self-Determination Act (1975), the Indian Health Care Improvement Act (1976), the Indian Child Welfare Act (1978), and the Indian Religious Freedom Act (1978). All these are positive events in the history of American Indians. It is, however, very difficult for American Indians to forget the treatment they received from whites and to believe that a period of termination or relocation will not come again. Thus American Indians are still very suspicious of white people and tend to mistrust anyone outside their society (particularly whites) who make promises concerning socioeconomic, political, and cultural opportunities.

Mental health professionals interested in working with American Indians should be familiar with the overall effects of the above historical events in the lives of American Indians. This guideline is particularly relevant for white mental health professionals who, during the process of assessment and treatment, may feel that they are being rejected or mistrusted by an American Indian client without apparent reasons.

The Indian Child Welfare Act (ICWA). Practitioners involved in the assessment and treatment of Indian children must have "extensive knowledge of the Indian Child Welfare Act [passed by the U.S. Congress in 1978] and its implications for the client system" (Goodluck, 1993, p. 222). This act " . . . acknowledged the tribe as the best agency to determine custody issues for Indian children. The Act reaffirmed that tribes possessed jurisdiction over child-custody proceedings for all Indian children living on the reservation" (O'Brien, 1989, p. 212). In addition, the ICWA states that if an Indian child resides off-reservation or in a Public Law 280 state (a state with the authority to use its civil and criminal laws on reservations), the state court is required to transfer jurisdiction to the tribal court unless the parents object to this requirement (O'Brien, 1989). A therapist should not handle court actions involving child abuse, foster care, and adoption among American Indian families in the absence of extensive knowledge and applicability of the ICWA.

The basic elements of this act are (Goodluck, 1993)

- Child custody proceedings (e.g., procedures for defining a child as Indian, tribal court jurisdiction, placement standards, and returning the child to tribal jurisdiction)
- Indian child and family program development (provides information for tribes interested in developing service programs for Indian children)
- Record keeping and information (procedures for disclosure of information, Indians' rights, and benefits)

Familism

Like African Americans, Hispanics, and Asians, the extended family has primacy among American Indians; the self is secondary. The self (individual) is also secondary with respect to the role of the tribe (Richardson, 1981). In comparison with Hispanics and Asians, American Indians place more emphasis on the administration of the family by the father and older relatives than on authority (Asians) or *machismo* (Hispanics). Mutual respect between wife and husband, between parents and children, between family members and relatives, and between family members and the tribe is highly rewarded (Ho, 1992; Matheson, 1986; Richardson, 1981).

Strong family relationships are emphasized, but a sense of independence among family members is rewarded, particularly among children and adolescents (Ho, 1992). For example, American Indian children are rarely told directly what to do and are often encouraged to make their own decisions. Few rules are best among American Indians; if rules exist, they must be flexible and loosely written (Richardson, 1981). This cultural value includes the administration of the family and children by parents, relatives, and tribe leaders. It is particularly important for therapists to avoid looking for the "head" of the family with the authority to make decisions regarding the entire family during the assessment and treatment of American Indians. Contrary to Asian and Hispanic fathers, the father (or older adults) in American Indian families only "administers" the family; he does not control the family in the sense of being "authoritarian" or *macho*.

An important cultural value among American Indians' perception of familism is the consultation of tribal leaders, the elderly, and the medicine man or woman when marital conflicts emerge. This is particularly important in cases when husband and wife are from two different tribes and the main conflict involves the discipline of their children. If the therapist suspects that such conflicts may be the result of different values, norms, or beliefs, an elder from either tribe should be consulted to clarify cultural differences between the two tribes and the contribution of such differences in the manifestation of these conflicts.

Sharing and the Concept of Time

Everything must be shared among American Indians, including the solution to problems, material goods, and time (Ho, 1992). American Indians treats time as a natural event and do not believe that time should control their natural way of living (Ho, 1992). Time among many American Indians is not used as a measuring tool (i.e., hours, minutes) but rather is related to holistic task (McDonald, 1994). The event (task) rather than the clock is what is important among many American Indians. (Sue & Sue, 1990, suggest that a similar concept of time may be held by many Hispanics, in which the task or event has primacy over time.)

In the same way that material goods must be shared, many American Indians believe that time (to fulfill a given task) must also be shared with others. For example, an American Indian client may be late for his or her therapy session not because he or she wants to be late or is resistant to the therapy, but because on the way to the clinic the client met a friend and spent time talking about family matters, business, or other issues. In this example, the task (e.g., the client's social contact with that friend) is more important than punctuality (i.e., the clock). Questioning this particular client about being late would be a bad strategy and a sign that the therapist is not familiar with the way time is used by American Indians.

Nonverbal Communication

Like Asians, American Indians place great emphasis on nonverbal forms of communication. Listening is more important than talking among American Indians (Matheson, 1986; Richardson, 1981). American Indians believe that one can learn a great deal just by listening to what other people are saying. Thus American Indians communicate feelings and emotions through clues with their bodies, eyes, and tone of voice. An American Indian client who seems quiet during the therapy session is actually listening and attending very carefully to the therapist's verbal remarks. Similarly, when the client is talking, he or she expects the therapist to listen and to attend to both verbal and nonverbal cues. When the client perceives that the therapist is listening, this perception is translated into a recognition that the therapist understands the problem and that he or she may have good suggestions for the solution of that problem.

Two special forms of nonverbal communication are the lack of eye contact and a slight handshake. In western culture, eye contact is a sign of respect and attention to others. For many American Indians, however, eye contact is a sign of disrespect. "Forcing" an American Indian client to look directly in the eyes of the therapist could make the client very uncomfortable (Thompson et al., 1993). As noted Johnson, Fenton, Kracht, Weiner, and Guggenheim (1988), American Indians generally press hands with a slight touch and believe that a firm handshake represents a sign of aggression. Failure to appreciate these cultural distinctions may lead to error in the diagnosis of many American Indian clients. For example, an American Indian client who avoids eye contact and a firm handshake, and who generally shows other nonverbal communication styles considered in western culture as *psychomotor retardation*, could easily be diagnosed with depression (Johnson et al., 1988).

Individualism

Like Hispanics and Asians, American Indians reject the traditional sense of individualism leading to competition among family members and between American Indians and other people (Richardson, 1981). American Indians may be seen as unmotivated, lazy, and unproductive because they do not share American individualism. Among American Indians, the emphasis is on collectivism and the sense of working together to achieve common goals among all members of the tribe; but a recognition of the qualities of the individual and his or her independence is also emphasized (O'Brien, 1989). Therapists need to understand the implicit harmony between the rights of an individual's self-actualization versus the tribal's actualization and/or survival (McDonald, 1994).

A failure to recognize the implicit harmony between individualism and collectivism among many American Indians could lead to failure in the assessment and treatment of this group. For example, if during the process of psychotherapy an American Indian client believes that the therapist is recommending a procedure or technique that may lead to discord and disharmony among family and tribal members, that client will not follow through with that recommendation (Sue & Sue, 1990).

The First Session

Recognize Limited Understanding of American Indians' Culture and the Positive Feeling of Being an Indian

If the therapist is not American Indian, he or she should begin the first session with a clear statement regarding his or her limited understanding regarding cultural values, religions, and traditions among American Indians. The therapist should also verbally state that he or she would like the client to correct any error or offensive statement based upon the therapist's lack of understanding of the client's culture and values (Richardson, 1981). In addition, during this session it is appropriate to let American Indian clients know that their history shows that they are good people and that they should feel proud of themselves.

Avoid Pseudosecrecy Statements and Do Not Ask Questions Unrelated to the Core Clinical Problem

The therapist should avoid statements such as "Feel free to tell me . . ." or "You can rest assured I will not discuss your problems with . . ." As noted by Richardson (1981) and Walker and LaDue (1986), American Indians have heard these statements many times from the great white father and the federal bureaucrats; each time American Indians have been deceived.

Similarly, questions unrelated to the core problems should be avoided. For example, it may not be appropriate to ask an American Indian client "What does your father think about the restriction on hunting?" or "Why don't Indians share the same tradition in the management of children across tribes?" These questions would be considered offensive by American Indians (Richardson, 1981).

Do Not Discuss Medication

During the first meeting, it is particularly important for the therapist to avoid statements dealing with the use of medication to treat the problem. Synthetic medication is not good for the health of Indians.

Accept Relatives, Friends, Medicine Man/Woman, Tribal Leader

The therapist should not be surprised if the client brings unexpected people to the first meeting. American Indians do not mind sharing their emotional problems with their relatives, friends, tribal leader, and the medicine man or woman (Richardson, 1981).

Avoid Taking Many Notes

An American Indian client wants the therapist to listen; taking notes is a sign of not listening and disrespect. Taking notes makes the process of the interview more formal and structured, which is the opposite of American Indians' belief in simplicity and flexibility during social contacts with other people (Ho, 1993; Richardson, 1981). If the therapist must take notes, he or she should ask permission from the client and remember to summarize these notes at the end of the session to indicate that he or she understood the main concern. If the therapist senses note taking is not acceptable (through nonverbal signals from the client), then he or she should show to the client (nonverbally) that it is acceptable not to take notes.

Listen Rather Than Talk

Many American Indian clients come to see a therapist because they want the therapist to listen to what they have to say about the core clinical problem; these clients do not come to therapy to listen to the therapist. Thus it is important that the therapist use his or her ears rather than mouth during the first session with an American Indian client.

Confidentiality Versus Resistance

During the first session, an American Indian client from a small community may not want to answer questions dealing with his or her personal or private life. This attitude may be erroneously considered as resistance from the client and mistrust toward the therapist. The client, however, may be aware that relatives or friends may work in the hospital or clinic and will not answer such questions for fear that his or her answers will be entered in the medical record and become public (Thompson et al., 1993). Thus, if after hearing an overall statement concerning confidentiality (which is always recommended with clients from all multicultural groups) the client refuses to answer such questions, the appropriate approach is not to label the client's behavior as resistance but to consider it as a sign indicating that issues of confidentiality have not been resolved. The second approach is to ask the client directly if he or she is aware of a relative or friend working in that hospital or clinic. If the answer is yes, the client should be allowed to make his or her own decision regarding the best way to handle this situation. Making a promise to an American Indian client regarding confidentiality may be a bad tactic. Only the client would know whether such relatives and friends should be trusted.

Explore Important
Potential Problems

During the first session with American Indian clients, the therapist should place particular attention on the screening of alcoholism and depression symptoms. Alcoholism is not only the primary concern among American Indians, but it also is considered the main cause of suicide and violence in this group (O'Brien, 1989; Walker & LaDue, 1986). The therapist should also screen American Indian women for symptoms of alcoholism to prevent fetal alcohol syndrome (a disease that produces severe physical, social, and intellectual deficits among children of alcoholic women).

Feelings of inadequacy and low self-esteem are indications of depression in this group. These feelings have been associated with the negative impact of reservations and Indian boarding schools (Walker & LaDue, 1986). In addition, stress and other emotional problems are often associated with relocation (i.e., moving out of the reservations and to urban areas). Therefore it is important to determine whether or not the client recently moved from a reservation. An American Indian client who sees himself or herself as affected by these events would benefit by discussing these events with a therapist who can understand the development of such events and their dramatic effects on the lives of American Indians, particularly during the Manifest Destiny and assimilation periods.

Conducting Psychotherapy

Traditional Healers and
Mental Health Professionals

The use of traditional healers (e.g., the medicine man or woman) in the interpretation and solution of problems among American Indians is increasing among American Indians living in urban areas and reservations (Matheson, 1986; Richardson, 1981; Walker & LaDue, 1986). Thus many American Indian clients seeking professional help for their mental health disorders expect the professional to be familiar and ready to integrate traditional healing practices with western healing practices.

A list of legitimate healers could greatly enhance the process of the therapist's credibility (as described in Chapter 2). This list may be obtained from local Indian boards and specialized institutions such the Dull Knife Memorial College (see Table 6.1). In fact, clinicians (in particular non- Indian practitioners) should encourage American Indian clients to consult traditional healers in the Indian communities and to discuss ways to integrate western and traditional healers during the course of assessment and treatment (Thompson et al., 1993). (It is important to emphasize that although American Indian healers often practice healing to control evil spirits, these healers do not generally practice black magic or witchcraft, i.e., the use of the healing process to harm others; Thompson et al., 1993.)

Thompson et al. (1993) suggest that it would be inappropriate to question American Indians about details involving specific procedures used by Indian healers. Many American Indians believe that if those procedures "are to be revealed at all to non-Indians, or even to someone from another tribe, it is only after a long and trusting relationship has been established" (p. 208).

Recommended Modalities of Therapies

Following are guidelines recommended for all forms of psychotherapy conducted with American Indian clients (Ho, 1993; Thompson et al., 1993; Walker & LaDue, 1986).

First, for many Indians the present is more important than the future. The practitioner should be able to screen this perception of time quickly to determine whether therapy should be present-oriented.

Second, many American Indians believe that it is disrespectful to ask a lot of questions; when American Indians ask questions during psychotherapy, the function of such questions is to clarify instructions given by the therapist.

Third, basic survival issues and unmet needs in the American Indian family or client under treatment should be explored by using a nondirective approach. Moving from the reservation to an urban area, unemployment, medical complications, and poverty are examples of survival issues and unmet needs that may lead to violence, heavy drinking, and marital problems.

Fourth, once the potential impact of survival issues and unmet needs has been explored, a directive problem-solving approach is recommended in which the therapist suggests a concrete and feasible solution to problems. The assistance of the medicine man or woman may be combined with the problem-solving approach.

Fifth, many American Indian clients expect some clarification concerning the cause(s) of their problems and what exactly they can do to deal with such problems from mental health professionals. This expectation requires considerable time and flexibility on the part of the therapist.

Sixth, for American Indian clients who travel great distances to see a therapist, it is important to have a plan to encourage subsequent visits to the clinic and facilitate the effects of treatment. The following points should be considered in that plan (Thompson et al., 1993): use of self-help groups close to the client's residence; recruitment of the healthiest members of the family as "cotherapists" (instructed to assist with the use and monitoring of the therapist's instructions at home); and use of brief therapy with short-term objectives.

Behavioral Approaches

Behavioral approaches are recommended with American Indian clients because these approaches emphasize the cause of behavior (including maladaptive behavior) as determined primarily by external events and avoid explanation of behavior in terms of internal conflicts (Walker & LaDue, 1986). An important element in behavioral approaches for American Indians is the emphasis on environmental events leading to disruptions in an important aspect of the survival pact: the symbiotic relationship between the environment and the individual or the group. Similarly, many American Indians believe that problems in the individual and the group can result from a disruptive individual/group-environment relationship caused by the effects of negative events in their lives (e.g., epidemics, reservations, Indian boarding schools). Behavioral approaches teach clients how to establish better relationships with the environment by making viable decisions in the presence of external (negative) events and by modifying external behavior-consequence relationships leading to changes in behavior (Walker & LaDue, 1986).

Family Therapy

Many American Indian families believe that a client is experiencing a family problem (e.g., marital problems, difficulties in handling children, school problems) because the family does not have the ability to provide essential needs, including food, shelter, and health to their members (Ho, 1993). If family therapy is recommended with this group, it is important to deal with the family's basic needs initially, including the provision of advice regarding the fulfillment of these needs. The therapist should have available a listing of social agencies specializing in American Indians and should discuss this list with the family. This approach shows that the therapist is sensitive to the family's basic needs and that he or she is able to provide immediate delivery of services, which in turn could lead to the enhancement of the family-therapy therapeutic relationship.

During the family therapy process, additional guidelines include the following (Ho, 1993).

1. The therapist should emphasize group decision making by involving all nuclear and extended family members (including the medicine man or woman and tribal leaders).

2. All suggestions given to the family should be presented in a concrete, slow, and calm mode, which indicates that the therapist is sensitive to flexibility and the time-oriented approach among American Indians.

3. The therapist should determine the tribal identity of the family and whether all members involved in the family belong to the same tribe. This guideline is particularly important in cases when the family's problem involves conflicts between husband and wife regarding the management of their children. For example, in the Hopi tribe the wife is the one primarily responsible for the management of children, whereas in the Cherokee tribe the discipline of children is shared by both husband and wife. Thus a Cherokee woman who marries a Hopi man would show marital discord if her husband shows no concern regarding the discipline of their children (see Ho, 1992, pp. 154-155).

4. The therapist should allow family members to decide what exactly they want to manage during the process of family therapy. For example, an American Indian family might come to family therapy seeking help in how to fulfill some basic needs. When these needs are met, that family might terminate therapy. If the same family returns for additional family therapy sessions (after those basic needs have been met), this is a sign that family members believe it is time to deal with relationship problems and reasons for the initial contact to the clinic. These reasons could include marital problems, school difficulties, and alcoholism (Ho, 1993).

Group Therapy

A common belief is that group therapy is not appropriate for American Indians. However, several scholars believe that this observation is not totally true. Manson, Walker, & Kivlahand (1987), McDonald (1994), and Thompson et al. (1993) recommend the use of group therapy with American Indian clients (particularly in the prevention and management of alcoholism), especially when it is programmed in combination with traditional Indian activities. In addition, Manson et al. (1987) point out that it is appropriate to recommend group therapy with American Indian clients because this intervention "is an outgrowth of the natural emphasis on groups in the social ecology of most Indian and Native communities" (p. 170). Three specific guidelines should be remembered when group therapy is programmed with American Indian clients (Sue & Sue, 1990; Thompson et al., 1993).

1. Support and/or permission from tribal officials should be obtained before scheduling group therapy.
2. If the therapist is not an American Indian, he or she should conduct group therapy with the assistance of American Indian professionals (e.g., Indian social workers, teachers, school counselors, psychologists, psychiatrists).
3. The medicine man or women, tribal leaders, elders, and other respected tribal members should be invited to particularly actively in some group therapy sessions (members of the group should be consulted regarding the applicability of this recommendation; they may provide suggestions to determine the selection of tribal members with high status in the tribe).

Medication

The use of medication in the treatment of mental disorders among Indian people has not been systematically studied or reviewed. However, Thompson et al. (1993) note that most classes of psychotropic medication are effective with this group. The therapist should remember to avoid discussions involving the possibility of drug therapy during the first meeting with an American Indian client.

Psychodynamic Model

For many American Indians, mental problems are the result of external events rather than the result of internal conflicts or difficulties with an individual. In general, psychodynamic psychotherapy does not take into account environmental events and places heavy emphasis upon internal conflicts. Thus this approach is not recommended with American Indian clients (Walker & LaDue, 1986).

Treatment of Children

Regardless of the sort of treatment used, if an Indian child is the client, the most important guideline to remember is to avoid giving recommendations to parents that appear to indicate that the child is being forced to behave or not to behave in a certain way. A "rightness of choice" (Ho, 1987, p. 77) is expected among Indian children, and the main task for parents is to assist their children in making the right choice. Thus a treatment plan with emphasis on ordering, verbal reprimands, and threats is not recommended in the management of Indian children.

Foster Care and Adoption

Before making decisions regarding the placement of Indian children in foster care or adoption, the therapist should remember that the Indian Child Welfare Act provides that Indian families have preference in making that decision. That is, a clinician should not make decisions regarding foster care and adoption without consultation with the tribe and parents (O'Brien, 1989; Thompson et al., 1993). This guideline is particularly important to remember in cases when such decisions include the placement of Indian children with non-Indian families.

Organizations for American Indians

Because of the number of policies and regulations (some from the government, others from the tribes) among American Indian communities, the therapist should consult with organizations specialized in these communities to enhance the process of assessment and treatment of American Indian clients. Examples of these organizations are listed in Table 6.1. Readers interested in a quick reference regarding these policies and regulations across Indian tribes are encouraged to consult *American Indian Tribal Governments* (O'Brien, 1989).

7

Guidelines for the Prevention of Attrition
With African American, American Indian,
Asian, and Hispanic Clients

Attrition is generally defined as a client's failure to return for therapy. It is estimated that 50% of culturally diverse groups terminate therapy after only one contact with a mental health professional (Boyd-Franklin, 1989; Marin & Marin, 1991; Sue & Sue, 1990; Wilkinson & Spurlock, 1986; Yamamoto, 1986)). Several strategies are recommended to prevent attrition, including telephone calls and letters to remind the client about subsequent therapy sessions, greeting cards (e.g., Christmas cards), reduction in the cost of therapy, and changes in the schedule for therapy to accommodate the client's own schedule.

However, these strategies do not seem to work with culturally diverse groups. An appropriate approach to prevent attrition in these groups would be an emphasis on a client's cultural variables and the impact of these variables upon attrition. Attention to the guidelines in this text could dramatically reduce attrition among multicultural groups. The following tables present summaries of the guidelines, recommended in the prevention of attrition during the process of psychotherapy, from prior chapters. These tables emphasize general guidelines in the prevention of attrition

Table 7.1 General Guidelines in the Prevention of Attrition

1. Make sure that the client finds what he or she is looking for (e.g., acceptance of the client's belief system).
2. The client expects a quick solution to problem.
3. Explore the client's expectation regarding therapy.
4. Involve extended family members (biological and nonbiological members) in the assessment and treatment process. With Asian clients, issues of shame and humiliation may preclude the inclusion of nonbiological members in the assessment and treatment of the client.
5. Explain the reason(s) for reducing the length and frequency of treatment sessions to avoid a perception of lack of interest in working with a given group.
6. If paraprofessionals are used, do not use them too frequently or the client may feel that he or she is being treated as a "second class" client (because he or she is not often seen by professionals).
7. Use a modality of therapy that is directive, active, and structured, and provide a tentative solution to the core problem (particularly during the first session).
8. Use mental health professionals (e.g., psychologists, psychiatrists, social workers) and supporting staff (e.g., secretaries, receptionists) with cross-cultural training.

(Table 7.1), followed by specific guidelines recommended in treating African Americans (Table 7.2), Hispanics (Table 7.3), Asians (Table 7.4), and American Indians (Table 7.5). The generalization of one or more of these guidelines across groups should be considered in cases when the clinician believes that a guideline for one group may apply in the case of other groups.

Table 7.2 Guidelines for Preventing Attrition of African American Clients

1. Discuss racial differences.
2. Avoid linking mental problems with parents' behaviors; these problems result from environmental conflicts in society.
3. Do not try to know about family secrets by questioning the client regarding these secrets.
4. Assure the client that the church can be included in the assessment and treatment of the case.
5. Do not recommend medication as the first treatment choice; this is an impersonal treatment that may suggest that the therapist does not want to work with the client.
6. The therapist should not give the impression that he or she is the protector of the race when discussing racial issues.
7. Referrals made by schools or social welfare agencies may be seen by the client as a threat to his or her autonomy. Discuss this feeling with the client.

Table 7.3 Guidelines for Preventing Attrition of Hispanic Clients

1. Use *formalismo* (formalism) during the first contact with the client, but gradually move to *personalismo* (personalism) in subsequent contacts.
2. Assure the client that the church can be included in the assessment and treatment of the client.
3. Conduct a brief interview with the father to recognize his authority in the family.
4. Talk about spiritual events leading to emotional problems (e.g., *mal puesto*, or hex; *mal de ojo*, or evil eye).
5. Do not provide suggestions that may compete with the belief in *machismo* and *marianismo*.
6. During the first session, ensure that the client leaves the clinic with recommendations regarding how to handle the problem; avoid the impression that more information is needed in subsequent sessions to provide these recommendations.
7. Because medication is expected, discuss the possibility of prescribing medication during the first and subsequent sessions.
8. Time is not a fundamental variable; do not ask a client reasons for being late for therapy.

Table 7.4 Guidelines for Preventing Attrition of Asian Clients

---

All Asian Clients:

1. Avoid personalism; clients expect an emphasis on formalism during the entire process of therapy.

2. Disclose educational background to ensure credibility and a sense that the client is with a competent therapist.

3. Do not force or encourage the client to reveal his or her problems; wait until the client is ready to discuss these problems. Shame and humiliation suppress the public admission of problems among many Asians.

4. Do not recommend the independence of children from their families (particularly their parents).

5. Avoid a discussion of hospitalization of the client without considering other alternatives (e.g., home treatment).

Southeast Asian Clients:

6. Provide social service referrals (e.g., housing, school).

7. Consider a discussion of traumatic events (e.g., deaths in the family during the war) carefully. A premature discussion of these events could lead to additional stress, which could increase the probability of attrition.

Table 7.5 Guidelines for Preventing Attrition of American Indian Clients

---

1. Emphasize listening rather than talking.

2. Time is not a fundamental variable; do not ask the client reasons for being late for therapy.

3. Recommend therapies leading to a sense of "working together" to achieve a common goal; competition is not allowed.

4. Avoid pseudosecrecy statements.

5. Synthetic medication is not expected, particularly during the first session.

6. Avoid therapies emphasizing "order" and "authority" (e.g., "I want you to do . . ."; "You should learn how to control . . .")

7. Talk about the "administration" of the problem rather than the "control" of the problem.

8. Avoid personalism.

8

Guidelines for Evaluating and Using the Epidemiological Mental Health Literature With Multicultural Groups

A central issue in the assessment and treatment of multicultural groups is the therapist's ability to evaluate critically and use data on the epidemiology of psychiatric disorders or mental problems with these groups. The overall methodology in collecting epidemiological data is to take a sample from a given population (e.g., a sample of African Americans, Hispanics), to screen that sample in relation to a particular variable or event (e.g., schizophrenia, depression, phobias), and then to calculate a particular score for that sample. This score is used to estimate the *prevalence* (the current frequency of that event or variable at the moment the sample was screened) and *incidence* (number of new cases) of that event or variable. The score, translated into a prevalence or incidence score, is used to make generalizations about the manifestation of that particular variable or event (e.g., the prevalence and incidence of depression) in the population from which the sample was drawn.

When practitioners read the epidemiological mental health literature involving multicultural groups, the first conclusion they encounter is that the prevalence and incidence of mental disorders is higher among African

Americans, Hispanics, Asians, and American Indians than it is among whites and other ethnic groups in this country (e.g., Greek, Italian, Irish, Polish Americans). Among African Americans, Hispanics, Asians, and American Indians, the literature suggests that both the prevalence and the incidence of mental disorders is higher in the African American community (Escobar, 1993).

Practitioners must avoid making generalizations from the literature regarding the assessment and treatment of culturally diverse groups in their daily clinical practices. Three reasons support this guideline: a lack of uniformity in the definition of mental problems or psychiatric disorders across epidemiological studies; a lack of cultural validity in most epidemiological studies; and biases in reporting the epidemiology of mental health within culturally diverse groups.

No Uniform Definitions of Mental Disorders

Investigators have not yet agreed upon a single instrument to measure mental disorder in psychiatry epidemiology; no uniform definitions of mental disorder exist in studies investigating the prevalence and incidence of this psychiatric disorder (Neighbors & Lumpkin, 1990). For example, Koslow and Rehm (1991) list 21 instruments that investigators could use to assess the prevalence and incidence of depression in children and adolescents (e.g., Children's Depression Inventory, Children's Depression Scale, the Schedule for Affective Disorders and Schizophrenia for Children— Kiddie-SADS, and the Depression Scale Modified for Children). This problem of multiple instruments to measure the same disorder is noted in the assessment of depression in adults, as well as with respect to other mental disorders (e.g., conduct disorder, attention deficit hyperactivity disorder, schizophrenia, personality disorders) among both younger and older populations. Thus epidemiological studies using different instruments in the assessment of prevalence and incidence of mental disorders may yield different results across studies when the instruments do not share the same items, the same number of items, or the same cutoff score (i.e., the score used to determine presence of "depression" versus "nondepression").

Thus when practitioners read "black children have been found to exhibit the highest rates of childhood psychopathology and psychiatric impairment" (Ho, 1992, p. 80), or that "prevalence of schizophrenia was found to be highest among African Americans, intermediate among [whites], and lowest among Hispanics" (Escobar, 1993, p. 55) and similar statements involving culturally diverse groups (Robins & Regier, 1991), they must remember that these statements are linked to results obtained from a particular instrument, and that when a different instrument is used to measure the same event, similar results may not result.

Because of the lack of an instrument that provides a uniform definition of mental disorders across studies, researchers have no choice but to use available instruments, which are at least reliable and valid in methodological terms (not necessarily in cultural terms). Researchers are expected to address this limitation (i.e., the uniformity of definition) when discussing the applications of their results in clinical practice.

Lack of Cultural Validity

To determine whether an investigator considers the impact of culture in the interpretation of data summarizing the epidemiology of mental health, the practitioner should read a study with the following question in mind: Does the study report about the potential effects of language, folk beliefs, and acculturation in the interpretation of data? If the study does not include sufficient materials to answer this question, it is probably culturally invalid.

The Effect of Language

Some data suggest that bilingual multicultural clients may be rated as being more psychopathological when they are interviewed in English than when they are interviewed in their native language. Marcos, Alpert, Urcuyo, and Kesselman (1973) asked mental health professionals to rate videotapes of Hispanic clients communicating in Spanish and Hispanic clients communicating in English. The raters detected more psychopathology during the English interview. These authors suggest that when bilingual culturally diverse clients are instructed to speak using English rather than their native language, they may appear tense, uncooperative, and more emotionally withdrawn.

Martinez (1986) points out that many Hispanic clients who speak minimal or no English first think in Spanish, then translate into English to themselves, and finally respond to the therapist in English. Many changes in the client's verbal and nonverbal behavior during this process may be interpreted as psychopathological. For example, Hispanic clients with little command of Standard American English would answer a question or remark from a therapist with a simple and restricted verbal output that may be interpreted as a case of "impoverishment of thought." In addition, looking for the right word or sentences in English can create anxiety leading to "thought derailment" or "loosening of association" (Martinez, 1986, p. 71).

Similar observations have been made about the potential effect of Nonstandard American English versus the effect of Standard American English on the evaluation of psychopathology. Russell (1988) cites a study in which white and African American therapists observed an actor (playing the role of a client) describing his mental problems in Black English and Standard American English. The study found that black therapists reported less psychopathology when the actor spoke in Black English and more psychopathology when the actor spoke in Standard English; the inverse findings were reported by white therapists.

Another important point to consider is whether code switching was allowed during the interview. This phenomenon is defined as "a total or partial language shift with a given situation or conversation" (Russell, 1988, p. 35). Code switching may allow a person to be more or less (depending on the nature of the interview) emotionally distant from important issues in the understanding of the problem under consideration (Pitta, Marcos, & Alpert, 1978; Yamamoto et al., 1993). Although code switching generally has been associated with bilingual clients in psychotherapy, the same phenomenon has been observed in African Americans who begin to use Black English several minutes into the interviewing process, perhaps to provide more information or to become emotionally divorced from the topic under consideration (Russell, 1988).

Three guidelines are recommended to determine whether a study considered the potential effect of language during the collection of epidemiological data.

1. The interview was conducted in the interviewee's language (e.g., Spanish) or the potential effect of the second language was considered in the interpretation of the results.

2. The interviewee was allowed to use Nonstandard American English to facilitate both process and content during the interview (e.g., African Americans were interviewed in Black English; see Russell, 1988, and Yamamoto et al., 1993, p. 113).

3. Code switching was allowed during an interview with bilingual or Nonstandard American English-speaking interviewees.

The Effect of Folk Beliefs

Beliefs in spirits, hexes, and other unseen events are culturally accepted among some members of the four multicultural groups described in this text. If those beliefs are not considered during the formulation of a clinical diagnosis, the client may be erroneously diagnosed with a psychiatric disorder. For example, if a Hispanic client reports that "An evil eye coming from people I know must be responsible for my bad behavior," a clinician unfamiliar with the place of evil eye (*mal de ojo*) in the client's belief system would erroneously conclude that this client is demonstrating a delusion that may lead to a diagnosis of schizophrenia (Martinez, 1986). Similarly, if certain items on the Minnesota Multiphasic Personality Inventory (MMPI) such as "Evil spirits possess me at times" are not viewed in the context of clients' beliefs, the outcome of the clinical interview would be that the client is mentally ill rather than that the item may represent an assessment of a belief that is culturally accepted by the client and those who share the same cultural background (Malgady, Rogler, & Constantino, 1987). When reading the mental health epidemiological literature, practitioners should look for a description of the potential impact of folk beliefs upon results indicating prevalence or incidence of psychiatric disorders among multicultural groups, particularly the Hispanic population.

The Effect of Acculturation

As noted by Dana (1993a), acculturation is a fundamental variable in the interpretation of clinical interview and psychological test data. In the evaluation and interpretation of psychiatric epidemiological data, practitioners are encouraged to screen whether a particular study considered the potential effect of acculturation in the interpretation of the data. If the study did not include a measure of acculturation and failed to report the potential impact of this variable during the collection of data, it is probably culturally invalid. For example, results obtained with the Developmental Inventory of Black Consciousness (DIB-C) and the Racial Identity Attitude Scale (RIAS), recommended to measure acculturation among African Americans, have been related to elevations on the MMPI scales of F (higher scores suggesting greater psychopathology or deviant response sets), 6 (paranoid), 8 (schizophrenia), and 9 (hypomania; Dana, 1993a). Similarly, Hispanics tend to receive higher MMPI profiles in cases when acculturation is not taken into consideration in the interpretation of such profiles (Dana, 1993a; Montgomery & Orozco, 1985). The same results have been reported with the Rosebud Personal Opinion Survey (Hoffmann, Dana, & Bolton, 1985), which is recommended to measure acculturation among American Plains Indians (for a summary of the Plains culture see Brandon, 1989, pp. 320-349, and Force & Force, 1991, pp. 50-53).

An example of lack of cultural validity in a major study in psychiatric epidemiology is the Epidemiologic Catchment Area Study (ECA; Robins & Regier, 1991). The major ECA report does not consider the potential impact of acculturation in the interpretation of the data involving African Americans and Hispanics (mainly Mexican Americans; Robins & Regier, 1991). In addition, only the Los Angeles ECA site, among five ECA sites, included a measure of acculturation, but only for Mexican Americans (Burnam et al. 1987). Burnam et al. (1987) selected items from the Acculturation Rating Scale for Mexican Americans (Cuellar et al., 1980) and the Behavioral Acculturation Scale (Szapocznik, Scopetta, Aranalde, & Kurtines, 1978) and found that "consistent with the acculturation findings, native-born Mexican Americans, who tended to have high levels of acculturation, had higher lifetime prevalence of disorders (phobias, alcohol abuse or dependence, drug abuse or dependence, as well as major depression and dysthymia) than immigrant Mexican Americans [i.e., the least acculturated group]" (p. 89). Table 8.1 presents examples of acculturation scales across the four multicultural groups described in this book; these scales should be included in an epidemiological study to determine the impact of acculturation on the data collected from these groups.

Biases in Reporting the Epidemiology of Mental Health

The above discussion emphasizes two issues that affect the nature of psychiatric epidemiological data: lack of a uniform definition of mental disorders and lack of cultural validity. Once the collection of data has been completed, researchers translate the data into prevalence and incidence scores. When these scores are reported, biases may occur in the actual reporting of the data. Practitioners must determine under what specific circumstances the reporting of psychiatric epidemiological data involving culturally diverse groups is biased. This task may be very difficult to fulfill by practitioners or clinicians who are extremely busy with their clients and with little time for careful reading of the literature. Three guidelines will help practitioners quickly screen biases in reports of epidemiological data collected with culturally diverse groups.

Table 8.1 Acculturation Scales

Name of Scale	Group	Reference
Acculturation Questionnaire	Vietnamese, Nicaraguan refugees	Smither & Rodriguez-Giegling (1982)
Acculturation Rating Scale for Mexican Americans	Mexican Americans	Cuellar et al., (1980)
Acculturative Balance Scale	Mexican Americans, Japanese	Pierce, Clark, & Kiefer (1972)
Behavioral Acculturation Scale	Cubans	Szapocznik, Suopetta, Arnalde, & Kurtines (1978)
Children's Acculturation Scale	Mexican Americans	Franco (1983)
Cuban Behavioral Identity Questionnaire	Cubans	Garcia & Lega (1979)
Cultural Life Style Inventory	Mexican Americans	Mendoza (1989)
Developmental Inventory of Black Consciousness	African Americans	Milliones (1980)
Ethnic Identity Questionnaire	Japanese Americans	Masuda, Matsumoto, & Meredith (1970)
Multicultural Acculturation Scale	Southeast Asians, Hispanic Americans, Anglo Americans	Wong-Rieger & Quintana (1987)
Multicultural Experience Inventory	Mexican Americans	Ramirez (1984)
Racial Identity Attitude Scale	African Americans	Helms (1986)
Rosebud Personal Opinion Survey	American Indians	Hoffmann, Dana, & Bolton (1985)
Suinn-Lew Asian Self-Identity Acculturation Scale	Chinese, Japanese, Koreans	Suinn et al., (1987)

1. Identify the sample (number of African Americans, Hispanics, etc.) from which the data were collected.
2. Determine the population (i.e., how many people in the entire population) from which the sample was selected to reach conclusions regarding the representativeness of the sample (e.g., Is this sample of African Americans representative of the population of African Americans in this country?).
3. Carefully read the conclusions of the study, which summarize major findings in words rather than in complex statistical procedures.

If the sample is too small or does not actually represent the particular group under study, the investigator is probably biased in reporting the data. That is, the investigator is assuming that the data can be generalized to the entire population from which that sample was selected, when in fact this may not be true.

The above point can be illustrated with the ECA Study, which has been considered "a landmark in psychiatric epidemiology" (Escobar, 1993, p. 51). In this study (Leaf, Meyers, & McEvoy, 1991), 19,182 people ranging in age from 18 years to 65 years and above were interviewed across five major U.S. cities between 1978 and 1986 (Baltimore, Durham, New Haven, Los Angeles, and St. Louis). Escobar (1993) summarizes several important results of this study, including that lifetime prevalence of schizophrenia, manic disorders, and phobias was higher among African Americans than among whites and Hispanics; that the prevalence of alcoholism among younger males was highest among Hispanics and whites and lowest among African Americans, but that among older males (age 45 and older) African Americans had the highest lifetime prevalence rate (i.e., having the symptoms any time during an individual's lifetime) for alcoholism; and that the lifetime prevalence rate for major depression was higher among whites than among Hispanics and African Americans. In one of the key papers on this study, Robins, Helzer, Weissman, Orvaschel, Gruenberg, Burke, & Regier (1984) conclude that "we might be tempted to infer from these . . . results in the northeast, mid-atlantic, and mideastern areas that there is little regional variation in the lifetime prevalence of these disorders in the United States" (p. 957). Keith, Regier, and Rae (1991), summarizing findings on schizophrenic disorders, conclude that they "found a somewhat higher rate of schizophrenia in the U.S. population than rates found in community studies in Europe. . . . We can have considerable confidence in these rates *because of the large sample*" (p. 52, italics added).

Another example of generalized statements in reporting data from this study is that "lifetime, one-year, and one-month prevalence rates for Hispanic men are higher than for the other two groups [i.e., whites and African Americans]" (Helzer, Burnam, & McEvoy, 1991, p. 86). Similar generalized statements regarding the results can be found in a summary for other psychiatric disorders (Robins & Regier, 1991).

Could the results of the ECA be generalized to the entire population of African Americans and Hispanics in the United States? Probably not. First, lifetime prevalence rates were based on a small number of cases across subsamples. In the study, the number of African Americans across sites ranged from 157 to 1,497 and the total (all sites) was 4,638 (10.4% of the total sample). The number of Hispanics ranged from 17 to 1,458 and the total was 1,600, or 5.5 % of the total sample (Leaf et al., 1991). In 1980 (when most data were collected), the total number of African Americans in the United States between the ages of 15 and 65 years and older was approximately 18.4 million (U.S. Bureau of the Census, 1992) and the total number of Hispanics in the same age range was approximately 15 million. Thus the ECA study included 0.02% of African Americans and 0.01% of Hispanics from the total number of these groups in 1980. These percentages did not represent the population of African Americans and Hispanics in 1980. Thus studies reporting prevalence of psychiatric disorders in African Americans and Hispanics using the ECA data set (e.g., Robins et al., 1984) may be considered as biased if they fail to mention that readers should consider the results with caution because of the small number of cases in both groups.

In addition, Leaf et al. (1991) report that a total of 1,600 Hispanics were included in the ECA data set. As noted by Escobar (1993), however, Hispanics represented in the study were largely Mexican Americans. In fact, in the Los Angeles site, 93% of the respondents were Mexican Americans. Thus extrapolation of the ECA conclusions to other Hispanics in the United States (e.g., Cubans, Dominicans, Puerto Ricans) could be interpreted as bias (Escobar, 1993). For example, the conclusion that "lifetime . . . prevalence rates [alcoholism] for Hispanic men are higher than for the other two groups" (Helzer, Burnam, & McEvoy, 1991, p. 86) would only apply to Mexican Americans.

It should be noted that some ECA investigators have recognized that the results were rarely statistically significant because of the small subsample sizes (Karno & Golding, 1991, p. 211; Robins et al., 1984, p. 955). In addition, some ECA investigators have also pointed out that a major limitation in that study was that the sample of Hispanics included mainly Mexican Americans and that the other two major Hispanic groups (Cubans and Puerto Ricans) were underrepresented (Leaf, Myers, & McEvoy, 1991). However, most studies summarizing the ECA data do not explicitly discuss these limitations.

In the case of the collection of mental health epidemiological data involving American Indians, an example of bias is provided by Thompson et al. (1993). Data from the Indian Health Service (IHS, created in 1955 as part of the U.S. Public Health Service to provide health care for Indians) "are widely quoted as being representative of all Indians" (Thompson et al., 1993, p. 199). A major bias in the reporting of such data is that the IHS only recognizes as Indians those living on 32 reservations, which means that Indians from other reservations (approximately 246) and those living in urban areas are not included in IHS statistics. Thompson et al. (1993)

also point out that "some tribes are *not recognized* by the federal government and, therefore, are not included in most statistics" (p. 199). If the sample (which includes only those Indians recognized by the federal government) is not representative of the majority of Indians in the continental United States, a certain degree of bias can be inferred in the report of such data.

Practitioners should read mental health epidemiological literature with the following guidelines in mind. First, granted that the absence of an uniform definition of mental disorder is an inherent problem in current research, a study should use reliable and valid instruments and discuss limitations in the generalization of the data in clinical practice because of that definitional problem. Second, the practitioner should determine the cultural validity of the study (e.g., a discussion regarding the impact of language upon the data). Third, the practitioner should determine whether the study included an assessment of acculturation. Fourth, the practitioner should check the population from which the sample was selected and determine whether this sample was representative of that population. Finally, the practitioner should read the conclusions of the study to identify potential biases regarding the generalization of results from the sample to the entire population.

9

_____

_____

____

Using Culturally Biased Instruments

Inaccuracies in the assessment and diagnosis of mental disorders can have three consequences: overdiagnosis, underdiagnosis, and misdiagnosis. Biases in testing are generally considered determinant factors in such inaccuracies. Many attempts have been made to eliminate or control biases in the assessment and diagnosis of multicultural groups, including the translation of tests into the language of the group being tested and the development of culturally appropriate norms (Westermeyer, 1993; Yamamoto, 1986). Despite these attempts, the overall sense among researchers and clinicians is that biases in cross-cultural testing still exist (Anastasi, 1988; Dana, 1993a). Flaherty, Gaviria, Pathak, Michell, Wintrob, Richman, & Birz (1988) point out that culture-free tests (i.e., a test that is not biased against specific culturally diverse groups) must fulfill five validity criteria.

1. Content equivalence (Are items relevant for the culture being tested?)
2. Semantic equivalence (Is the meaning of each item the same in each culture?)
3. Technical equivalence (Is the method of assessment comparable across cultures?)
4. Criterion equivalence (Would the interpretation of variables remain the same when compared with the norm for each culture studied?)

5. Conceptual equivalence (Is the test measuring the same theoretical construct across cultures?)

Currently, researchers and clinicians lack a test or assessment of any kind that could fulfill these criteria (Escobar, 1993). This suggests that culture-free tests are not yet available in the assessment of the four multicultural groups discussed in this book.

However, researchers and clinicians agree that, despite the reality of bias with most tests or instruments, it is important to use such tests in part because they provide a common language in the assessment and diagnosis of psychiatric disorders (Yamamoto, 1986). In addition, in terms of reimbursement and institutional requirements, many such tests are required in the clinical practice of therapists involved in the assessment and treatment of mental problems. Therefore it would be a bad strategy to advise practitioners to stop using these tests or instruments because they are biased (Dana, 1993a). A better strategy is to recognize that it is not practical to recommend that practitioners should throw out everything that is biased in the process of assessment of multicultural groups (Pedersen, 1993), and to determine "how best to utilize [these tests] with patients from a different cultural background" (Yamamoto, 1986, p. 116).

The literature suggests at least 10 guidelines that practitioners may use to minimize bias during the assessment and diagnosis of multicultural groups using current tests or instruments (Bulhan, 1985; Jenkins & Ramsey, 1991; Wilkinson & Spurlock, 1986).

1. The practitioner should examine his or her own bias and prejudice before engaging in the evaluation of clients who do not share the practitioner's race and ethnicity (see Chapter 1 for the distinction between race and ethnicity concepts).
2. The practitioner should be aware of the potential effects of racism.
3. The practitioner should include an evaluation of socioeconomic variables and use them.
4. The practitioner should try to reduce the sociocultural gap between the client and himself or herself.
5. The practitioner should include an evaluation of culturally related syndromes.
6. The practitioner should ask culturally appropriate questions.
7. The practitioner should consult paraprofessionals and folk healers within the particular multicultural group.
8. The practitioner should avoid the mental status examination.
9. The practitioner should try to use the least biased assessment strategies first, then consider the most biased strategies under special circumstances.

10. The practitioner should use Dana's (1993a, 1993b) assessment model as an overall approach to minimizing biases.

Examine Biases and Prejudices

Biases in assessment and diagnosis of culturally diverse groups may not necessarily be related to the particular strategy of assessment, but to bias and prejudices from the practitioner conducting that assessment (Jenkins & Ramsey, 1991). Thus it is important for practitioners to make a self-evaluation of the possibility of bias and prejudice in themselves before dealing with biased assessment strategies. Jenkins and Ramsey (1991) propose a set of questions dealing with the possibility of bias and prejudice among practitioners interested in working with African American clients. Any one of such questions receiving a "not at all" rating (in a very much, somewhat, not at all format) "means that the therapist is not yet ready to counsel African-American [clients] effectively" (p. 735). These questions may also be considered with other multicultural groups. Several questions have been added to these questions to assist practitioners in their evaluation of their own bias and prejudice.

Table 9.1 shows examples of such questions. Materials in this table could be further modified and extended with traditional questions from a practitioner's own clinical practice. The rating scale is numbered from 1 (very much) to 3 (not at all). To determine the overall utility of such questions in a self-assessment of potential bias and prejudice, add all the numbers for all items and divide them by the total number of questions to obtain a bias-prejudice ratio with a given multicultural group. For example, if number 1 is checked across all questions dealing with African American clients, the total score will be 10 and the ratio will be 1.0 (or 10/10). This score suggests that the person is probably free of bias and prejudice and ready to conduct assessment and diagnosis with these clients. As the score increases, the potential for bias and prejudice also increases. A score of 3.0 suggests a high level of bias and prejudice; a practitioner receiving this score should either refer the client to another clinician or obtain consultation from other professionals, paraprofessionals, or folk healers within the particular group. A similar assessment of bias and prejudice could be programmed with staff (e.g., other mental health professionals, paraprofessionals, secretaries). The scores obtained from staff could be used to determine whether cross-cultural training is necessary.

Table 9.1 Self-Evaluation of Biases and Prejudices

Question	1 (Very much)	2 (Somewhat)	3 (Not at all)
1. Have you had formal training with:			
African Americans	1	2	3
American Indians	1	2	3
Asians	1	2	3
Hispanics	1	2	3
Whites	1	2	3
2. Do you have cultural knowledge of:			
African Americans	1	2	3
American Indians	1	2	3
Asians	1	2	3
Hispanics	1	2	3
Whites	1	2	3
3. As a parent, would you approve of your son or daughter dating:			
African Americans	1	2	3
American Indians	1	2	3
Asians	1	2	3
Hispanics	1	2	3
Whites	1	2	3
4. Would you date or marry a member of the following group?			
African Americans	1	2	3
American Indians	1	2	3
Asians	1	2	3
Hispanics	1	2	3
Whites	1	2	3
5. Do you have a repulsion for or feel ill at ease with:			
African Americans	1	2	3
American Indians	1	2	3
Asians	1	2	3
Hispanics	1	2	3
Whites	1	2	3
6. Have you been exposed to professional views of:			
African Americans	1	2	3
American Indians	1	2	3
Asians	1	2	3
Hispanics	1	2	3
Whites	1	2	3

Table 9.1 (Continued)

Question	1 (Very much)	2 (Somewhat)	3 (Not at all)
7. Are you familiar with the current literature (journals, books, periodicals) of:			
African Americans	1	2	3
American Indians	1	2	3
Asians	1	2	3
Hispanics	1	2	3
Whites	1	2	3
8. Would you feel uncomfortable if you have a problem understanding:			
African Americans	1	2	3
American Indians	1	2	3
Asians	1	2	3
Hispanics	1	2	3
Whites	1	2	3
9. Would you expect favorable therapy with:			
African Americans	1	2	3
American Indians	1	2	3
Asians	1	2	3
Hispanics	1	2	3
Whites	1	2	3
10. Would you expect a favorable therapeutic relationship with:			
African Americans	1	2	3
American Indians	1	2	3
Asians	1	2	3
Hispanics	1	2	3
Whites	1	2	3

Group	Total Score	(Ratio)*
African Americans	_____	( )
American Indians	_____	( )
Asians	_____	( )
Hispanics	_____	( )
Whites	_____	( )

*For example, if 1 is checked for all questions involving African Americans, the total score would be 10 and the ratio would be 1.0 (or 10 divided by 10). The maximum bias-prejudice ratio is 3.0, suggesting a high degree of bias and prejudice toward a given group.

Be Aware of the Potential
Effects of Racism

When the prevalence and incidence of psychiatric disorders and intelligence test results are explained in terms of differences among races, this explanation is termed *racism*. An emphasis upon racism as an "explanation" in this context is considered a fundamental bias because it prevents practitioners from exploring more plausible explanations for a phenomenon (De La Cancela, 1993).

For example, intelligence test results are generally lower among African Americans, American Indians, Asians, and Hispanics than among whites (Jenkins & Ramsey, 1991). Diagnoses of schizophrenia are more frequently used with African American clients than with white clients (Wilkinson & Spurlock, 1986). In both cases, the main assumption is that race plays a fundamental role in the explanation of intelligence test results and the application of diagnostic categories involving multicultural groups. However, when other factors are considered (e.g., social background, income, educational level), significant differences between whites and culturally diverse groups are not apparent (Escobar, 1993; Jenkins & Ramsey, 1991). If a practitioner makes the mistake of emphasizing racism as explanation, he or she may make another error: the overdiagnosing of culturally diverse groups (e.g., "seeing" schizophrenia in an African American client simply because he or she is an African American).

Racism can also lead to underdiagnosis and misdiagnosis. For example, depression has been reported more frequently in white clients than in African American clients (Wilkinson & Spurlock, 1986). However, African American clients who are depressed may be underdiagnosed because the literature indicates that depression in this group is not as common as depression in the white population or because of the "myth that African Americans could not . . . become depressed" (Griffith & Baker, 1993, p. 161). For example, complaints of headaches, backaches, and pains in the extremities are not considered as examples of symptoms for depression in many diagnostic instruments, such as the Diagnostic and Statistical Manual of Mental Disorders (DSM-III-R; American Psychiatric Association, 1987). However, these symptoms may suggest depression in an African American client (Wilkinson & Spurlock, 1986, p. 23).

Similarly, depression among Asians may be underdiagnosed because of the tendency of this group to display somatic symptoms of depression (e.g., weight loss) and not because of their race per se (Yamamoto et al., 1993). Asians also tend to show a lower prevalence and incidence of psychiatric disorders in the epidemiological literature (Jenkins & Ramsey,

1993); this finding is probably related to the cultural value of shame that prevents Asians from making public their problems (Sue & Sue, 1990). In this finding, the Asian status may be irrelevant.

Autism is rarely diagnosed among African American children in comparison with white children. Wilkinson and Spurlock (1986) suggest that "there is a strong probability that instead of [autism] being rare, it frequently may be diagnosed erroneously as mental retardation" (p. 22). If true, this is another example of misdiagnosis.

Race seems to play a major role in the manifestation of mental health in the above examples. If the client is white, mental problems A, B, and C are expected (according to mental health epidemiological data). Similarly, if the patient is African American, mental problems D, E, and F are expected. This conclusion may "reflect biases in the assignment of diagnosis according to race" (Wilkinson & Spurlock, 1986, p. 17).

Include and Use an Evaluation
of Socioeconomic Variables

During the first session with African American, American Indian, Asian, and Hispanic clients, practitioners often collect social/economic data (e.g., income level, urban versus rural locations, parents' education, prenatal care, parenting, contacts with welfare agencies). During the clinical assessment and the assignment of the particular diagnosis, however, socioeconomic variables are rarely considered. Yet mental health problems frequently are more prevalent and have a higher incidence in lower socioeconomic families (Jenkins & Ramsey, 1991; Wilkinson & Spurlock, 1986, p. 22; Yamamoto, 1986, p. 108). Many members of the four multicultural groups discussed in this book are from low socioeconomic families. An assessment of these groups without taking into consideration socioeconomic variables could lead to bias in the assignment of diagnoses.

For example, studies assessing the mental health status of Vietnamese refugees reveal that symptoms of depression are noted when the head of the family does not have a job (Yamamoto, 1986, p. 108). This observation has been confirmed with other multicultural groups. For example, in the Hispanic Health and Nutrition Examination study (Escobar, 1993), Puerto Ricans were not only the most socioeconomically disadvantaged among Hispanics (in comparison with Mexican Americans and Cubans), but they also had a significantly higher prevalence of major depressive disorders.

Minimize the Sociocultural Gap

Some findings suggest that inaccuracies in the assessment and diagnosis of mental disorders may be the result of a difference between the therapist's and the client's sociocultural background (Jackson, Berkowitz, & Farley, 1974). In these findings, the greater the difference in sociocultural variables, the less accurate the assessment and diagnosis.

For example, African Americans often obtain lower scores on intelligence tests when these tests are administered by white practitioners rather than by African American clinicians (Jenkins & Ramsey, 1991). Other studies have shown that African Americans tend to alter their responses on self-report measures when the race of the examiner changes (Lineberger & Calhoun, 1983). Marcos (1976) suggests that when bilingual Hispanics clients are interviewed in English rather than in their native language, the probability of errors in assessment and diagnosis of psychiatric disorders may increase. Thus, to minimize biases in the assessment and diagnosis of culturally diverse groups using standard instruments, the practitioners should try to minimize the sociocultural gap between the himself or herself and the client.

Sue (1988) suggests that *ethnic match* seems more important than *racial match* in minimizing biases. This suggestion implies that if the examiner and the client do not share the same race but share similar values and lifestyles (e.g., a white examiner working with a highly acculturated Hispanic client), potential biases in the assessment and diagnosis of that client may be minimized. In this example, ethnic match (e.g., sharing similar values) seems more relevant than racial match (i.e., examiners and clients coming from the same racial group) in preventing bias. Sue (1988) also suggests that if examiners and clients are from the same racial group (e.g., Asian examiners and Asian clients) but do not share similar cultural values (e.g., acculturated Asian examiners versus recent Asian immigrants), biases in the assessment and diagnosis of such clients may increase. In this example, racial match seems less important than cultural match. Thus an emphasis upon ethnic match between examiners and clients is suggested to minimize bias in the assessment process.

Include an Evaluation of
Cultural-Related Syndromes

Culture-specific disorders are known as *cultural-bound syndromes* in the literature. Because many of these syndromes have been noted across different cultures, Simons and Hughes (1993) propose the term *cultural-related syndromes*.

Examples of cultural-related syndromes that practitioners are most likely to find in their practices include the following (Griffith & Baker, 1993; Rubel, O'Nell, & Collado-Ardon, 1984; Simons & Hughes, 1993).

- *Ataque de nervios* among Hispanics (out-of-consciousness state resulting from evil spirits)
- *Falling-out* in African American communities (seizurelike symptoms resulting from traumatic events such as robberies)
- *Ghost sickness* among American Indians (weakness, dizziness resulting from the action of witches and evil forces)
- *Hwa-byung* in Asian communities (pain in the upper abdomen, fear of death, tiredness resulting from the imbalance between reality and anger)
- *Koro* among Asians (a man's desire to grasp his penis resulting from the fear that it will retract into his body and cause death)
- *Taijin kyofusho* in the case of Asians (guilt about embarrassing others, timidity resulting from the feeling that the appearance, odor, facial expressions are offensive to other people)
- *Mal puesto,* hex, root-work, voodoo death among African Americans and Hispanics (unnatural diseases and death resulting from the power of people who use evil spirits)
- *Susto, espanto, pasmo, miedo* in the case of Hispanics (tiredness and weakness resulting from frightening and startling experiences)
- *Wacinko,* an American Indian's feeling of anger, withdrawal, mutism, suicide resulting from reaction to disappointment and interpersonal problems
- *Wind/cold* illness in the case of Hispanics and Asians (a fear of the cold and the wind; feeling weakness and susceptibility to illness resulting from the belief that natural and supernatural elements are not balanced)

Assuming that clinicians agree that it is important to consider the impact of cultural-related syndromes upon the assessment of multicultural groups, a crucial question is why such syndromes are not considered by clinicians in their clinical practices. There are two answers.

First, current standard clinical ratings and diagnostic instruments do not include criteria for the assessment of such syndromes. For example, clinical ratings such as the MMPI, the Child Behavior Checklist, and the Zung Depression Scale, as well as diagnostic instruments such as the DSM-III-R, do not require (and do not include) an assessment of such syndromes to distinguish between these syndromes and true psychopathology. Thus clinicians may not be concerned about screening cultural-related syndromes when making a diagnosis of mental disorders with a client from any of the multicultural groups discussed in this book. In the case of the DMS-III-R, practitioners are told that when using DSM-III-R criteria they should "assure that their use is culturally valid" (American Psychiatric Association, 1987, p. xxvi), but specific culturally valid criteria to guide the diagnosis of cultural-related syndromes are not given. It should be noted that in the preparation of the DSM-IV (scheduled for publication in 1994), experts have recommended more emphasis on the impact of cultural variables in the diagnosis of psychiatric disorders, as well as the inclusion of examples of culture-bound syndromes (Cervantes & Arroyo, 1994; Rogler, 1993). Major improvement, however, is not expected regarding the inclusion of cultural criteria across most psychiatric disorders in the DSM-IV (Rogler, 1993).

Second, reimbursement for clinical practices regarding cultural-related syndromes is not a practice among major private insurance, Medicaid, and Medicare. For example, a practitioner cannot expect to receive payment for the assessment and treatment of cultural-related syndromes such as *susto, ghost sickness, mal puesto, koro,* or *ataque de nervios.* A clinician in private practice would not be expected to spend time screening such syndromes in cases when his or her efforts will not lead to reimbursement.

A distinction should be made between considering the assessment of such syndromes only in cases when reimbursement for clinical assessment of such syndromes is available and the assessment of these syndromes because the clinician should ensure that a client is having a mental problem rather than a manifestation of cultural-related syndromes. The first point is a matter of money; the second is a matter of ethical standards leading to a recognition of cultural competence in the practice of a clinician involved in the assessment of multicultural groups. An important guideline to prevent unfair discriminatory practices and unethical behaviors in the assessment of African American, American Indian, Asian, and Hispanic clients is to have some familiarity with cultural-related syndromes shared by a particular group. In addition, the clinician should formulate a list of symptoms suggesting the presence of these cultural-related syndromes for consideration before a psychiatric diagnosis is applied to a particular client (American Psychological Association, 1992). Consultations with family members and peers within the particular groups should also be considered.

For example, if an American Indian client reports that "I believe that my weakness, loss of appetite, and fainting are the result of the action of witches and evil supernatural forces," this would be an example of schizophrenia to a clinician unfamiliar with the effect of ghost sickness among American Indians. If the client's belief is not shared by family members or peers, this belief is probably not a culturally supported belief (Westermeyer, 1993). Because current clinical ratings and diagnostic instruments do not include criteria for the assessment of such syndromes in clinical practice, practitioners must develop their own system of assessment of cultural-related syndromes.

Despite the importance of considering these cultural-related syndromes in clinical practice, too much emphasis on cultural-related syndromes may prevent practitioners from considering that many of these syndromes may include symptoms of severe psychiatric disorders. This emphasis not only could lead to misdiagnosis of real psychiatric disorders, but it may also result in turning clients over to folk healers for treatment under the assumption that a client has a cultural-related syndrome that cannot be treated by mental health professionals. As noted by Westermeyer (1993), turning multicultural clients over to folk healers because the presenting symptoms are examples of a cultural-related condition may lead to a major error in clinical practices. Thus the practitioner should assume that all cultural-related syndromes are potential cases for severe psychiatric disorders until further cross-cultural assessment reveals that culture is the major element in the manifestation of the syndromes. If culture is the major element in the syndrome, the client does not require psychiatric treatment.

Ask Culturally Appropriate Questions

During the interviewing process, a culturally appropriate line of questioning should be used to avoid misunderstanding and errors in the diagnosis of culturally diverse groups. This guideline can be illustrated by examples involving Asian clients, although similar examples might be generalized to other multicultural groups.

The questions "What is your opinion of yourself compared with other people?" and "Do you feel better, or not as good, or about the same as most?" are not always appropriate with Asian clients (Yamamoto, 1986, p. 112). In general, Asians do not like to compare themselves with other people. An Asian client may not answer the question, "Are you angry with your parents?" because he or she always shows respect toward parents (particularly the elderly), even if the relationship between a son or a daughter and parents is not good. Asian clients would not answer such questions. A practitioner unfamiliar with these cultural values would mistakenly use such values in the diagnosis of the client. In the first example, a more appropriate question would be, "Do you like yourself?" or "Do you feel okay about yourself as a person?" (Yamamoto, 1986,

p. 112). In the second example, Gaw (1993b) suggests the question "How is the relationship between you and your [parents]?" (p. 274).

Consult Paraprofessionals and
Folk Healers Within a Multicultural Group

Bias in the assessment and diagnosis of culturally diverse clients can be minimized if the clinician is assisted in that process by people within a particular group. The ideal strategy would be to include mental health professionals from the multicultural group. However, this strategy is difficult to implement because of the shortage of African American (1.2%), American Indian (0.2%), Asian (1.0%), and Hispanic (0.7%) mental health professionals (Russo, Olmedo, Stapp, & Fulcher, 1981). A practical and more realistic strategy is to use paraprofessionals and folk healers within the particular multicultural group.

For example, Southeast Asian clients sometimes feel insecure or threatened in unfamiliar settings (e.g., the office of a white therapist), which may lead to suspicion or mistrust resembling paranoid symptoms (Westermeyer, 1993). A paraprofessional Southeast Asian could quickly indicate that these symptoms are expected in refugees who have experienced repressive regimes and survived concentration camps.

In the case of African American and Hispanic clients, consultation with the *espiritista* or *curandero* or *folk healer* is recommended in cases when clients are evaluated with the MMPI and check "true" on items such as "Evil spirits possess me at times," "I believe I am being plotted against," and "I believe I am a condemned person." According to the profiles of the MMPI, these items are examples of individuals who exhibit paranoid or schizophrenic symptoms. However, these items may be endorsed by African Americans and Hispanics who generally believe in evil spirits, the action of witches, and malevolent supernatural powers (Martinez, 1986).

Because of the central role of the medicine man or woman among American Indian clients, these healers should always be consulted before reaching conclusions regarding the diagnosis and treatment of these clients (Walker & LaDue, 1986, pp. 176-177).

Avoid the Mental Status Examination

Clinicians often use the mental status exam to reinforce clinical data obtained with standard clinical rating and diagnostic instruments. This exam makes the assumption that a series of "normal" behaviors and cognitive processes are shared by "normal" people, regardless of cultural background. However, this assumption could dramatically multiply the impact of existing bias in current clinical ratings and diagnostic instruments (Hughes, 1993). The following examples of components of the mental status examination and their potential bias when used with multicultural groups may explain why it may be appropriate to avoid the mental status examination with multicultural groups (Hughes, 1993; Mueller, Kiernan, & Langston, 1992; Westermeyer, 1993).

During the assessment of concentration and vigilance, clients receive the Serial 7s Test, where the client is asked to subtract 7 from 100 and then to continue subtracting 7 from each answer. If the client has a problem in mastering this task, an assumption of anxiety, depression, and schizophrenia is formulated. If this assumption is "confirmed" with scores derived from a clinical rating scale, the practitioner would think that he or she is on the right track. Aside from the fact that the validity of this test is questioned by many researchers (see Hughes, 1993, pp. 27-28), many members of multicultural groups would fail because they are not versed in the area of counting forward or backward.

The assessment of orientation allows clinicians to assess negativism, confusion, distraction, hearing impairment, and receptive language disorders. This test emphasizes the assessment of the self (the person), place, and time. For example, a therapist could ask "What is your last name?" "What is the name of this month?" "Where are you right now?" In response to the first question, a Hispanic client may look confused and distracted because he or she would have to decide which last name of the two last names often used by Hispanics to report (Hispanics often have one last name from the father, e.g., Rodriguez, and another from the mother, e.g., Arias, such as Federico Antonio Rodriguez Arias). If the client is not familiar with the name of that month in Standard American English or is not familiar with the name of the building (or cannot remember that name), and he or she appears to provide an incorrect answer, the practitioner would assume that the client is exhibiting negativism, hearing impairment, or receptive language disorder.

The assessment of general knowledge can be used to evaluate poor educational background, severe deterioration in intellectual functioning, and the ability to assess remote memory. For example, a clinician could ask "What are the colors of the American Flag?" "How far is it from Houston to Chicago?" "What are the names of three countries in Central America?" "Who is the president of the United States?" "Who was the last president of the United States?" "What is the total population of the United

States?" As noted by Hughes (1993), the answers to such questions imply geographical and public knowledge; many members of multicultural groups do not have this kind of knowledge for two reasons: They are too poor to travel (which is one way to answer some of these questions); and many members of such groups are illiterate (Westermeyer, 1993). In addition, clients with different cultural backgrounds would perform poorly on this test.

The assessment of thought process is a crucial area. For example, thought blocking is a sudden cessation of thought or speech that suggests schizophrenia, depression, and anxiety (Mueller et al., 1992). Clients who are not fluent in English might show thought blocking. Clients with little command of Standard American English would spend a great deal of time looking for the correct word, phrase, or sentence before answering a question; this could create anxiety resulting in thought blocking (Martinez, 1986). African Americans who use black English in most conversational contexts would also spend a great deal of time looking for a phrase or sentence in Standard American English when they feel that Standard American English is expected in certain circumstances (Dillard, 1973; Yamamoto et al., 1993).

Appearance is another important element in the mental status examination. For example, lack of eye contact, failure to stare directly into the therapist's eyes, and careless or bizarre dressing and grooming could point to signs of psychiatric disorders (Hughes, 1993). Asian Americans and many African Americans avoid eye contact and staring at people's eyes during social interactions (Hughes, 1993; Sue & Sue, 1990), partially because in such groups it is impolite to maintain eye contact or to look directly into the eyes of other persons. The therapist's definition of what is normal dressing and grooming may not be shared by a client who always comes to the therapist right after finishing a long working day as a garage mechanic. This client will probably look dirty, with a soiled face, hands, and nails, and a careless appearance.

To appreciate why multicultural groups may have difficulties with the components of the mental status examination and why such difficulties could increase bias in the assessment of these groups, try to picture yourself in the place of one of these groups and attempt to deal with the elements of that exam. Would you pass these tests? For example, subtract 7 from 100 and continue doing this until you get to the lowest number (can you mention this number as you read this line?). Studies suggest that normal subjects make between 3 and 12 errors on this test (Hughes, 1993). Now try the orientation test; could you name the location and the building you are in after you have experienced a panic attack in an unfamiliar city?

In the case of the general knowledge test, can you name the capital of three countries in the Middle East, the distance from New York to Los Angeles, the distance from the sun to the earth, the distance from your house to your parents' house, the colors in your state flag, and the main difference between the U.S. flag and the Malaysian flag? For the assessment of your thought process, pretend that you are not fluent in Spanish and visit Mexico City; would you take time to think about what you want to say before you open your mouth and say it? Will you look up and down, looking for the right phrase, word, or sentence before you order lunch? To determine what people may think about the way you dress, pretend that you are a Puerto Rican taxi driver in New York City and at 3:00 p.m. on a hot summer day you realize that you have your first appointment with the therapist and decide to keep your appointment; later you learn that the therapist made a note that you were probably depressed or psychotic because you dressed carelessly and had dirty nails and hands and a soiled face. Knowing that you did not have time to go home to take a shower, shave, and change clothes, would you return for a second appointment?

Try to Use the Least Biased Assessment Strategies First

A review of the literature suggests an order concerning the degree of bias across assessment strategies (Dana, 1993a; Jenkins & Ramsey, 1991). In summarizing that degree of bias, that order (from less to more bias as the number increases) would be:

1. Physiological assessment (e.g., the use of electrodermal activity in the assessment of psychopathology; Boucsein, 1992)
2. Direct behavioral observations (e.g., intervals during which African American and white children display attention to task materials; Anderson, 1988; Paniagua & Black, 1990)
3. Self-monitoring (e.g., clients record their own overt or covert behaviors such as obsessive thoughts and number of tasks completed, respectively)
4. Behavioral self-report rating scales (e.g., Fear Survey Schedule; Wolpe & Lang, 1964)
5. Clinical interview (which includes the mental status examination)
6. Trait measures (e.g., California Psychological Inventory; Dana, 1993a)
7. Self-report of psychopathology measures (e.g., MMPI, Beck Depression Inventory; Dana, 1993a)

8. Projective tests with structured stimuli (e.g., Tell-Me-A Story Test or TEMAS; Constantino, Malgady, & Rogler, 1988; Malgady, Constantino, & Rogler, 1984)

9. Projective tests with ambiguous stimuli (e.g., Rorschach test; Dana, 1993a)

All assessment strategies listed above have some degree of bias (Dana, 1993a; Jenkins & Ramsey, 1991). The important guideline to remember is to emphasize assessment strategies in which interpretations and speculations are minimized. For example, the level of interpretations and speculations is much greater with projective tests than with direct behavioral observations. Thus, in comparison with projective tests, bias might be greatly reduced when direct behavioral observations (or behavioral assessment strategies) are programmed to measure a particular event (e.g., number of times a depressed client refuses to eat or does not participate in social activities).

Some practitioners only use behavioral assessment in the evaluation of their clients (e.g., behavior analysts). The majority of practitioners, however, use a combination of trait measures, intelligence measures, self-report of psychopathology measures, and projective measures. If these measures are used, the practitioner should make an effort to select measures with evidence of cross-cultural validity. Table 9.2 includes examples of tests recommended with culturally diverse groups. Tests in Table 9.2 may minimize bias, but total elimination of biases is not expected (Dana, 1993a; French, 1993; López & Nunez, 1987). A review of these tests can be found in Dana (1993a).

Use Dana's Assessment Model

Dana (1993a, 1993b) provides an assessment model that clinicians may use in combination with the above guidelines in an overall approach to minimizing biases during the assessment of multicultural groups. Dana recommends five steps in the application of his model.

Conduct an Assessment of Acculturation

Dana emphasizes that the assessment of acculturation "should be administered and interpreted prior to application of any assessment procedures whatsoever" (1993b, p. 10). Chapter 8 includes examples of acculturation scales across the four multicultural groups discussed in this text.

Table 9.2 Tests Recommended With Culturally Diverse Groups

Name	Area	Reference
Center for Epidemiologic Studies Depression Scale (CES-D)	Depression	Radloff (1977)
Culture Fair Intelligence Test	Intelligence	Anastasi (1988)
Draw-A-Person Test (DAP)	Projective	French (1993)
Eysenck Personality Questionnaire (EPQ)	Personality	Eysenck & Eysenck (1975)
Holtzman Inkblot Technique (HIT)	Projective	Holtzman (1988)
Kaufman Assessment Battery for Children (K-ABC)	Intelligence	Kaufman, Kamphaus, & Kaufman (1985)
Leiter International Performance Scale	Intelligence	Anastasi (1988)
Progressive Matrices	Intelligence	Anastasi (1988)
Schedule for Affected Disorders and Schizophrenia (SADS)	Most Disorders	Spitzer & Endicott (1978)
System of Multicultural Pluralistic Assessment (SOMPA)	Intelligence	Mercer & Lewis (1978)
Tell-Me-A Story Test (TEMAS)	Personality/ Cognition	Constantino et al. (1988)

Provide a Culture-Specific Service Delivery Style

This step emphasizes the provision of "behavioral etiquettes" that facilitate a task-oriented approach and a trusting client-therapist relationship, necessary to initiate and complete the testing procedures. For example, with Hispanic clients the use of *Señor*, *Señora*, or *Señorita* in an environment including features (e.g., pictures, furniture) from that particular racial/ethnic group could greatly enhance the testing process.

Use the Client's Native Language (or Preferred Language)

For example, Hispanic and Asian American clients may be told "Perhaps you would feel more comfortable if we do this test in your native language.

If you prefer to do this test in English, please let me know about your preference."

Select Assessment Measures
Appropriate for the Cultural
Orientation and Client Preferences

Dana recommends the use of culture-specific instruments and an assessment process tailored to less acculturated clients. This guideline represents the *emic perspective* in the assessment of multicultural groups, which emphasizes an understanding of clients in their cultural context. For example, behavioral observation (either in the clinic or at home) would be recommended to understand how Hispanic families interact verbally and nonverbally. The use of life history reports may provide Asian, Hispanic, or American Indian clients with the opportunity to talk about their problems using culture-specific modes of communication (e.g., language, gestures). The tests listed in Table 9.2 are also recommended (see also Dana, 1993a, pp. 141-167).

Use a Culture-Specific Strategy
When Informing the Client About Findings
Derived From the Assessment Process

The applicability of this step can be illustrated by examples from the MMPI scales (Graham, 1990) and subscales from the Wechsler Adult Intelligence Scale—WAIS (Golden, 1990). (The same culture-specific strategy is recommended when reporting findings derived from other measures.) Parents of a Hispanic adolescent client could be told, "I understand that in the Hispanic culture, many people believe that they can be affected by evil spirits. Perhaps the finding with this test [e.g., MMPI] suggests that your son is expressing this cultural belief rather than being crazy" (meaning *loco*, which implies a more severe condition in the mind of many Hispanics). Similarly, an American Indian client may be told, "This finding suggests that you have low self-esteem, are reserved and timid, lack interest in activities, and that you are a shy person. My understanding is that among American Indians these behaviors are culturally accepted in their tribes. So, we probably need to talk more about these behaviors to ensure that they are not part of the clinical diagnosis of the mental problem you reported earlier to me."

The K-scale is one of the validity scales used to detect instances of test bias during the interpretation of results derived from the clinical scales of the MMPI profiles. An extremely low score on the K-scale suggests, among other things, that the client is skeptical and tends to be suspicious about the motivations of other people. Cultural paranoia could explain why an African American client has a low score on the K-scale. In the case of Asian clients, the expression of psychological problems in terms of somatic complaints is a culturally accepted phenomenon. For this reason, an elevation on the Hypochondriasis Scale (Hs) with Asian clients should be interpreted in terms of this cultural phenomenon.

Cuellar (1994) suggests that the client may not admit that he or she is actually suffering from a mental problem if given the option (e.g., in the presence of the MMPI scores) to interpret the problem in terms of cultural variables. Cuellar suggests that an alternative approach would be to sit down with the client and/or family members and discuss possible cultural explanations. On the basis of this informal discussion, the clinician could then decide if cultural variables explain test findings. In this recommendation, the opinion of the client and/or family members regarding the interpretation of test data in terms of cultural variables is minimal.

In the case of the WAIS (and the same test for children), Golden (1990) points out that this test "remains heavily influenced by cultural and language concepts that reflect the life of the average American, but not that of most [multicultural] groups" (p. 46). This observation is particularly true in the case of the performance by members of these groups on the information, comprehension, vocabulary, picture completion, and picture arrangement subtests, which are associated with alternate cultural backgrounds. For example, a Hispanic client may receive a very low score on the information subtest (e.g., below 5, where the mean is 10 and the standard deviation is 3) not because the client is not intelligent but because he or she lacks information regarding the total population, height of women, number of senators, and other "general knowledge" expected from the average American in the United States. A similar point can be made in the interpretation of scores from the comprehension (the client may not be able to understand basic U.S. customs and situation), vocabulary (the client cannot define a word using Standard American English), picture completion (the client cannot complete the picture because he or she is not familiar with objects pictured in the American culture), and picture arrangement (the client cannot arrange the pictures to tell a logical and coherent story because the social sequence is not part of the client's cultural background) subtests.

In each example, the task for the therapist engaged in the assessment of these groups (particularly Hispanics and Asians) will be to explain to his or her client the potential impact of cultural variables on these scores. For example, in the case of the vocabulary subtest, the therapist could say to a Hispanic client, "Your score on this test is very low. Perhaps you have problems communicating in English. I will repeat the same test using words from your own language" (translations of the WAIS are available in Spanish and other languages).

As noted by Golden (1990) and Sue and Sue (1990), many mental health professionals (particularly within the African American and Hispanic communities) have suggested that all Wechsler tests (and other individual intelligence tests such as the Stanford-Binet) are biased against multicultural groups (particularly African American and Hispanics). As noted in the beginning of this chapter, however, suggesting the exclusion of these tests from the practice of many clinicians is a bad tactic. Teaching practitioners how to interpret biased tests using cross-cultural skills seems more appropriate. For example, a low score on the information subtest could be used to suggest brain damage (Golden, 1990); however, a clinician with cross-cultural skills in this area would quickly point out that the client probably scored low on that subtest because he or she did not have the information expected from people familiar with the American culture.

References

Allen, A. (1988). West Indians. In L. Comas-Díaz & E. E. H. Griffith (Eds.), *Clinical guidelines in cross-cultural mental health* (pp. 305-333). New York: John Wiley.

American Psychiatric Association (1987). *Diagnostic and Statistical Manual of Mental Disorders* (3rd ed.). Washington, DC: American Psychiatric Association.

American Psychological Association (1992). *Ethical principles of psychologists and code of conduct.* Washington, DC: American Psychological Association.

Anastasi, A. (1988). *Psychological testing* (6th ed.). New York: Macmillan.

Anderson, L. P., Eaddy, C. L., & Williams, E. A. (1990). Psychosocial competence: Toward a theory of understanding positive mental health among black Americans. In D. S. Ruiz & J. P. Comer (Eds.), *Handbook of mental health and mental disorder among black Americans* (pp. 255-271). Westport, CT: Greenwood Press.

Anderson, W. H. (1988). The behavioral assessment of conduct disorder in black children. In R. L. Jones (Ed.), *Psychoeducational assessment of minority group children: A case book* (pp. 103-123). Berkeley, CA: Cobb & Henry.

Atkinson, D. R., & Wampold, B. E. (1993). Mexican Americans' initial preferences for counselors: Simple choice can be misleading—Comments on López, López, and Fong (1991). *Journal of Consulting Psychology, 40,* 245-248.

Baker, F. M. (1988). Afro-Americans. In L. Comas-Díaz & E. E. H. Griffith (Eds.), *Clinical guidelines in cross-cultural mental health* (pp. 151-181). New York: John Wiley.

Baker, F. M., & Lightfoot, O. B. (1993). Psychiatric care of ethnic elders. In A. C. Gaw (Ed.), *Culture, ethnicity, and mental illness* (pp. 517-552). Washington, DC: American Psychiatric Press.

Bamford, K. W. (1991). Bilingual issues in mental health assessment and treatment. *Hispanic Journal of Behavioral Sciences, 13,* 377-390.

Berg, I. K., & Jaya, A. (1993). Different and same: Family therapy with Asian-American families. *Journal of Marital and Family Therapy, 19,* 31-38.

Bernal, G., & Gutierrez, M. (1988). Cubans. In L. Comas-Díaz & E. E. H. Griffith (Eds.), *Clinical guidelines in cross-cultural mental health* (pp. 233-261). New York: John Wiley.

Berry, J. W., Pooringan, Y. H., Segall, M. H., & Darsen, P. R. (1992). *Cross-cultural psychology: Research and applications.* New York/Cambridge, UK: Cambridge University Press.

Betancourt, H., & López, S. R. (1993). The study of culture, ethnicity, and race in American psychology. *American Psychologist, 48,* 629-637.

Boucsein, W. (1992). *Electrodermal activity.* New York: Plenum.

Boyd-Franklin, N. (1989). *Black families therapy: A multisystems approach.* New York: Guilford.

Brandon, W. (1989). *Indians.* Boston: Houghton Mifflin.

Bulhan, A. H. (1985). Black Americans and psychopathology: An overview of research and theory. *Psychotherapy, 22,* 370-378.

Burnam, M. A., Hough, R. L., Karno, M., Escobar, J. I., & Telles, C. A. (1987). Acculturation and lifetime prevalence of psychiatric disorders among Mexican Americans in Los Angeles. *Journal of Health and Social Behavior, 28,* 89-102.

Canino, I. A., & Canino, G. J. (1993). Psychiatric care of Puerto Ricans. In A. C. Gaw (Ed.), *Culture, ethnicity, and mental illness* (pp. 467-499). Washington, DC: American Psychiatric Press.

Cervantes, R. C., & Arroyo, W. (1994). DSM-IV: Implications for Hispanic children and adolescents. *Hispanic Journal of the Behavioral Sciences, 16,* 8-27.

Chung, D. K. (1992). Asian cultural commonalities: A comparison with mainstream American culture. In D. K. Chung, K. Murase, & F. Ross-Sheriff (Eds.), *Social work practice with Asian Americans* (pp. 27-44). Newbury Park, CA: Sage.

Comas-Díaz, L. (1988). Cross-cultural mental health treatment. In L. Comas-Díaz & E. E. H. Griffith (Eds.), *Clinical guidelines in cross-cultural mental health* (pp. 337-361). New York: John Wiley.

Comas-Díaz, L. (1994, January). Personal communication with the author.

Comas-Díaz, L., & Duncan, J. W. (1985). The cultural context: A factor in assertiveness training with mainland Puerto Rican women. *Psychology of Women Quarterly, 9,* 463-476.

Comas-Díaz, L., & Griffith, E. E. H. (Eds.). (1988). *Clinical guidelines in cross-cultural mental health.* New York: John Wiley.

Constantino, G., Malgady, R. G., & Rogler, L. H. (1988). *Technical manual: The TEMAS thematic apperception test.* Los Angeles: Western Psychological Services.

Cook, K. O., & Timberlake, E. M. (1989). Cross-cultural counseling with Vietnamese refugees. In D. R. Koslow & E. P. Salett (Eds.), *Crossing cultures in mental health* (pp. 84-100). Washington, DC: International Counseling Center.

Costello, R. M., & Hays, J. R. (1988). *Texas law and the practice of psychology: A source book.* Austin: Texas Psychological Association.

Cuellar, I. (1994, January). Personal communication with the author.

Cuellar, I., Harris, L. C., & Jasso, R. (1980). An acculturation scale for Mexican American normal and clinical populations. *Hispanic Journal of the Behavioral Sciences, 2,* 199-217.

Dana, R. H. (1993a). *Multicultural assessment perspectives for professional psychology.* Boston: Allyn & Bacon.

Dana, R. H. (1993b, November 5). *Can "corrections" for culture using moderator variables contribute to cultural competence in assessment?*. Paper presented at the Annual Convention of the Texas Psychological Association, Austin, Texas.

De La Cancela, V. (1993). Rainbow warriors: Reducing institutional racism in mental health. *Journal of Mental Health Counseling, 15,* 55-71.

Dillard, J. L. (1973). *Black English: Its history and use in the United States.* New York: Vintage.

Escobar, J. E. (1993). Psychiatric epidemiology. In A. C. Gaw (Ed.), *Culture, ethnicity, and mental illness* (pp. 43-73). Washington, DC: American Psychiatric Press.

Eysenck, H. J., & Eysenck, S. B. S. (1975). *Manual for the Eysenck Personality Questionnaire.* San Diego, CA: Educational and Industrial and Testing Service.

Fairchild, H. H. (1985). Black, Negro, or African-American? The differences are crucial. *Journal of Black Studies, 16,* 47-55.

Flaherty, J. H., Gaviria, F. M., Pathak, D., Michell, T., Wintrob, R., Richman, J. A., & Birz, S. (1988). Developing instruments for cross-cultural psychiatric research. *Journal of Nervous and Mental Disease, 176,* 257-263.

Flaskerud, J. H., & Anh, N. T. (1988). Mental health needs of Vietnamese refugees. *Hospital and Community Psychiatry, 39,* 435-436.

Fleming, C. M. (1992). American Indians and Alaska Natives: Changing societies past and present. In M. Orlandi and R. Weston (Eds.), *Cultural competence for evaluators* (pp. 147-171). Rockville, MD: U.S. Department of Health and Human Services.

Force, R. W., & Force, M. T. (1991). *The American Indians.* New York: Chelsea House Publishers.

Foreman, J. (1993, June 6). Navajos refuse to panic over perplexing disease. *Houston Chronicle,* pp. 1, 18.

Franco, J. N. (1983). An acculturation scale for Mexican American children. *Journal of General Psychology, 108,* 175-181.

French, L. A. (1993). Adapting projective tests for minority children. *Psychological Reports, 72,* 15-18.

Fujii, J. S., Fukushima, S. N., & Yamamoto, J. (1993). Psychiatric care of Japanese Americans. In A. C. Gaw (Ed.), *Culture, ethnicity, and mental illness* (pp. 305-345). Washington, DC: American Psychiatric Press.

Garcia, M., & Lega, L. I. (1979). Development of a Cuban ethnic identity questionnaire. *Hispanic Journal of the Behavioral Sciences, 1,* 247-261.

Gaw, A. C. (1993a). *Culture, ethnicity, and mental illness.* Washington, DC: American Psychiatric Press.

Gaw, A. C. (1993b). Psychiatric care of Chinese Americans. In A. C. Gaw (Ed.), *Culture, ethnicity, and mental illness* (pp. 245-280). Washington, DC: American Psychiatric Press.

Golden, C. J. (1990). *Clinical interpretation of objective psychological tests* (2nd ed.). Boston: Allyn & Bacon.

Goodluck, C. T. (1993). Social services with Native Americans: Current status of the Indian Child Welfare Act. In H. P. McAdoo (Ed.), *Family ethnicity: Strength and diversity* (pp. 217-226). Newbury Park, CA: Sage.

Graham, J. R. (1990). *MMPI-2: Assessing personality and psychopathology.* New York: Oxford University Press.

Graves, T. D. (1967). Psychological acculturation in a tri-ethnic community. *Southwestern Journal of Anthropology, 23,* 337-350.

Griffith, E. E. H., & Baker, F. M. (1993). Psychiatric care of African Americans. In A. C. Gaw (Ed.), *Culture, ethnicity, and mental illness* (pp. 147-173). Washington, DC: American Psychiatric Press.

Griffith, E. E. H., English, T., & Mayfield, V. (1980). Possession, prayer, and testimony: Therapeutic aspects of the Wednesday night meeting in a black church. *Psychiatry, 43,* 120-128.

Harjo, S. S. (1993). The American Indian experience. In H. P. McAdoo (Ed.), *Family ethnicity: Strength in diversity* (pp. 199-216). Newbury Park, CA: Sage.

Helms, J. E. (1986). Expanding racial identity theory to cover the counseling process. *Journal of Counseling Psychology, 33,* 62-64.

Helzer, J. E., Burnam, A., & McEvoy, L. T. (1991). Alcohol abuse and dependence. In L. N. Robins & D. A. Regier (Eds.), *Psychiatric disorders in America: The epidemiologic catchment area study* (pp. 81-115). New York: Free Press.

Ho, M. K. (1992). *Minority children and adolescents in therapy.* Newbury Park, CA: Sage.

Ho, M. K. (1993). *Family therapy with ethnic minorities.* Newbury Park, CA: Sage.

Hoffmann, T., Dana, R., & Bolton, B. (1985). Measured acculturation and MMPI-168 performance of Native American adults. *Journal of Cross-Cultural Psychology, 16,* 243-256.

Holtzman, W. H. (1988). Beyond the Rorschach. *Journal of Personality Assessment, 52,* 578-609.

Hughes, C. C. (1993). Culture in clinical psychiatry. In A. C. Gaw (Ed.), *Culture, ethnicity, and mental illness* (pp. 3-41). Washington, DC: American Psychiatric Press.

Jackson, A., Berkowitz, H., & Farley, G. (1974). Race as a variable affecting the treatment involvement of children. *Journal of the American Academy of Child Psychiatry, 13,* 20-31.

Jackson, E. L., & Westmoreland, G. (1992). Therapeutic issues for black children in foster care. In L. A. Vargas & J. D. Koss-Chioino (Eds.), *Working with culture: Psychotherapeutic interventions with ethnic minority children and adolescents* (pp. 43-62). San Francisco: Jossey-Bass.

Jalali, B. (1988). Ethnicity, cultural adjustment, and behavior: Implications for family therapy. In L. Comas-Díaz & E. E. H. Griffith (Eds.), *Clinical guidelines in cross-cultural mental health* (pp. 9-32). New York: John Wiley.

Jenkins, J. O., & Ramsey, G. A. (1991). Minorities. In M. Hersen, A. E. Kazdin, & A. S. Bellack (Eds.), *The clinical psychology handbook* (pp. 724-740). New York: Pergamon.

Johnson, T. M., Fenton, B. J., Kracht, B. R., Weiner, M. F., & Guggenheim, F. G. (1988). Providing culturally sensitive care: Intervention by a consultation-liaison team. *Hospital and Community Psychiatry, 39,* 200-202.

Jones, A. C. (1992). Self-esteem and identity in psychotherapy with adolescents from upwardly mobile middle-class African American families. In L. A. Vargas & J. D. Koss-Chioino (Eds.), *Working with culture: Psychotherapeutic interventions with ethnic minority children and adolescents* (pp. 25-42). San Francisco: Jossey-Bass.

Joyce, P. R., & Paykel, E. S. (1989). Predictors of drug response in depression. *Archives of General Psychiatry, 46,* 89-99.

Karkabi, B. (1993, July 21). More than semantics: Heritage, image influence blacks' self-perception. *Houston Chronicle,* pp. 1D, 5D.

Karno, M., & Golding, J. M. (1991). Obsessive compulsive disorder. In L. N. Robins & D. A. Regier (Eds.), *Psychiatric disorders in America* (pp. 204-219). New York: Free Press.

Kaufman, S., Kamphaus, R. W., & Kaufman, N. L. (1985). New directions in intelligence testing: The Kaufman Assessment Battery for Children (K-ABC). In B. B. Wolman (Ed.),

Handbook of intelligence: Theories, measurements, and applications (pp. 663-698). New York: John Wiley.

Keith, S. J., Regier, D. A., & Rae, D. S. (1991). Schizophrenic disorders. In L. N. Robins & D. A. Regier (Eds.), *Psychiatric disorders in America: The epidemiologic catchment area study* (pp. 33-52). New York: Free Press.

Kim, L. I. C. (1993). Psychiatric care of Korean Americans. In A. C. Gaw (Ed.), *Culture, ethnicity, and mental illness* (pp. 347-375). Washington, DC: American Psychiatric Press.

Kim, S. C. (1985). Family therapy for Asian Americans: Strategic-structural framework. *Psychotherapy, 22,* 342-348.

Kim, S., McLeod, J. H., & Shantzis, C. (1992). Cultural competence for evaluators working with Asian-American communities: Some practical considerations. In M. Orlandi and R. Weston (Eds.), *Cultural competence for evaluators* (pp. 203-260). Rockville, MD: U.S. Department of Health and Human Services.

Kinzie, J. D., & Leung, P. K. (1993). Psychiatric care of Indochinese Americans. In A. C. Gaw (Ed.), *Culture, ethnicity, and mental illness* (pp. 281-304). Washington, DC: American Psychiatric Press.

Kolko, D. J. (1987). Simplified inpatient treatment of nocturnal enuresis in psychiatrically disturbed children. *Behavior Therapy, 2,* 99-112.

Koslow, D. R., & Salett, E. P. (Eds.). (1989). *Crossing cultures in mental health.* Washington, DC: International Counseling Center.

Koslow, N. J., & Rehm, L. P. (1991). Childhood depression. In T. R. Kratochwill & R. J. Morris (Eds.), *The practice of child therapy* (2nd ed.) (pp. 43-75). New York: Pergamon.

Kratochwill, T. R., & Bergan, J. R. (1990). *Behavioral consultation in applied settings: An individual guide.* New York: Plenum.

Lange, A. J., & Jakubowski, P. (1976). *Responsible assertive behavior.* Champaign, IL: Research Press.

Leaf, P. J., Myers, J. K., & McEvoy, L. T. (1991). Procedures used in the epidemiologic catchment area study. In L. N. Robins & D. A. Regier (Eds.), *Psychiatric disorders in America: The epidemiologic catchment area study* (pp. 11-30). New York: Free Press.

Lefley, P., & Pedersen, P. B. (Eds.). (1986). *Cross-cultural training for mental health professionals.* Springfield, IL: Charles C Thomas.

Levin, J. S., & Taylor, R. J. (1993). Gender and age differences in religiosity among black Americans. *The Gerontologist, 33,* 16-23.

Lineberger, M. H., & Calhoun, K. S. (1983). Assertive behavior in black and white American undergraduates. *Journal of Psychology, 113,* 139-148.

López, S., & Nunez, J. A. (1987). Cultural factors considered in selected diagnostic criteria and interview schedule. *Journal of Abnormal Psychology, 96,* 270-272.

López, S. R., López, A. A., & Fong, K. T. (1991). Mexican Americans' initial preferences for counselors: The role of ethnic factors. *Journal of Counseling Psychology, 38,* 487-496.

Malgady, R. G., Constantino, G., & Rogler, L. H. (1984). Development of a thematic apperception test (TEMAS) for urban Hispanic children. *Journal of Consulting and Clinical Psychology, 52,* 986-996.

Malgady, R. G., Rogler, L. H., & Constantino, G. (1987). Ethnocultural and linguistic bias in mental health evaluation of Hispanics. *American Psychologist, 42,* 228-234.

Manson, S. M., Walker, R. D., & Kivlahand, D. R. (1987). Psychiatric assessment and treatment of American Indians and Alaska Natives. *Hospital Community Psychiatry, 38,* 165-173.

Marcos, L. R., Alpert, M., Urcuyo, L., & Kesselman, M. (1973). The effect of interview language on the evaluation of psychopathology in Spanish-American schizophrenic patients. *American Journal of Psychiatry, 130,* 549-553.

Marin, G., & Marin, B. V. (1991). *Research with Hispanic populations*. Newbury Park, CA: Sage.

Martinez, C. (1986). Hispanic psychiatric issues. In C. Wilkinson (Ed.), *Ethnic psychiatry* (pp. 61-87). New York: Plenum.

Martinez, C. (1988). Mexican-Americans. In L. Comas-Díaz & E. E. H. Griffith (Eds.), *Clinical guidelines in cross-cultural mental health* (pp. 182-203). New York: John Wiley.

Martinez, C. (1993). Psychiatric care of Mexican Americans. In A. C. Gaw (Ed.), *Culture, ethnicity, and mental illness* (pp. 431-466). Washington, DC: American Psychiatric Press.

Martinez, R. E. (1993, August). Minority label "dehumanizing" [Letter to the editor]. *San Antonio Express News*, p. 5B.

Masuda, M., Matsumoto, G. H., & Meredith, G. M. (1970). Ethnic identity in three generations of Japanese Americans. *Journal of Social Psychology, 81*, 199-207.

Matheson, L. (1986). If you are not an Indian, how do you treat an Indian? In H. P. Lefley & P. B. Pedersen (Eds.), *Cross-cultural training for mental health professionals* (pp. 115-130). Springfield, IL: Charles C Thomas.

McAdoo, H. P. (Ed.). (1993). *Family ethnicity: Strength in diversity*. Newbury Park, CA: Sage.

McDonald, A. (1994, January). Personal communication with the author.

Mendoza, R. H. (1989). An empirical scale to measure type and degree of acculturation in Mexican-American adolescents and adults. *Journal of Cross-Cultural Psychology, 20*, 372-385.

Mercer, J., & Lewis, J. (1978). *System of multicultural pluralistic assessment*. New York: Psychological Corporation.

Mueller, J., Kiernan, R. J., & Langston, J. W. (1992). The mental status examination. In H. H. Goldman (Ed.), *Review of general psychiatry* (pp. 109-117). San Mateo, CA: Appleton & Lange.

Milliones, J. (1980). Construction of a black consciousness measure: Psychotherapeutic implications. *Psychotherapy: Theory, Research, and Practice, 17*, 175-182.

Mollica, R. F. (1989). Developing effective mental health policies and services for traumatized refugee patients. In D. R. Koslow & E. P. Salett (Eds.), *Crossing cultures in mental health* (pp. 101-115). Washington, DC: International Counseling Center.

Mollica, R. F., & Lavelle, J. (1988). Southeast Asian refugees. In L. Comas-Díaz & E. E. H. Griffith (Eds.), *Clinical guidelines in cross-cultural mental health* (pp. 262-293). New York: John Wiley.

Montgomery, G. T., & Orozco, S. (1985). Mexican Americans' performance on the MMPI as a function of level of acculturation. *Journal of Clinical Psychology, 41*, 203-212.

Moyerman, D. R., & Forman, B. D. (1992). Acculturation and adjustment: A meta-analytic study. *Hispanic Journal of Behavioral Sciences, 14*, 163-200.

Murase, K. (1992). Models of service delivery in Asian American communities. In D. K. Chung, K. Murase, & F. Ross-Sheriff (Eds.), *Social work practice with Asian Americans* (pp. 101-119). Newbury Park, CA: Sage.

Neff, J. A., & Hoppe, S. K. (1993). Race/ethnicity, acculturation, and psychological distress: Fatalism and religiosity as cultural resources. *Journal of Community Psychology, 21*, 3-20.

Neighbors, H. W., & Lumpskin, S. (1990). The epidemiology of mental disorder in black population. In D. S. Ruiz (Ed.), *Handbook of mental health and mental disorder among black Americans* (pp. 55-70). Westport, CT: Greenwood Press.

O'Brien, S. (1989). *American Indian tribal governments*. Norman: University of Oklahoma Press.

Paniagua, F. A., & Baer, D. M. (1981). A procedural analysis of the symbolic forms of behavior therapy. *Behaviorism, 9,* 171-205.

Paniagua, F. A., & Black, S. A. (1990). Management and prevention of hyperactivity and conduct disorders in 8-10 year old boys through correspondence training procedures. *Child and Family Behavior Therapy, 12,* 23-56.

Paniagua, F. A., Wassef, A., O'Boyle, M., Linares, S. A., & Cuellar, I. (1993). What is a difficult mental health case? An empirical study of relationships among domain variables. *Journal of Contemporary Psychotherapy, 23,* 77-98.

Pedersen, P. (1987). *Handbook of cross-cultural counseling and therapy.* Westport, CT: Greenwood Press.

Pedersen, P. (1993, April 16). Personal communication with the author.

Pierce, R. C., Clark, M., & Kiefer, C. W. (1972). A "bootstrap" scaling technique. *Human Organization, 31,* 403-410.

Pitta, P., Marcos, L. R., & Alpert, M. (1978). Language switch as a treatment strategy with bilingual patients. *The American Journal of Psychoanalysis, 38,* 255-258.

Radloff, L. S. (1977). The CES-D scale: A self-report depressions scale for research in the general public. *Applied Psychological Measurement, 1,* 385-401.

Ramirez, M. (1984). Assessing and understanding biculturalism-multiculturalism in Mexican-American adults. In J. L. Martinez & R. H. Mendoza (Eds.), *Chicano psychology* (pp. 77-94). Orlando, FL: Academic Press.

Ramirez, S. Z. (1994, January). Personal communication with the author.

Ramirez, S. Z., Paniagua, F. A., Linskey, A., & O'Boyle, M. (1993, August). *Diagnosing mental disorders in Hispanic children and youth: Cultural considerations.* Paper presented at the Annual Convention of the American Psychological Association, Toronto, Canada.

Ramirez, S. Z., Waseff, A., Paniagua, F. A., & Linskey, A. O. (1993, November). *The significance of cultural evaluations of psychopathology in ethnic minority individuals.* Paper presented at the Annual Convention of the Texas Psychological Association, Austin, Texas.

Ramirez, S. Z., Wassef, A., Paniagua, F. A., Linskey, A. O., & O'Boyle, M. (1994). Perceptions of mental health providers concerning cultural factors in the evaluation of Hispanic children and adolescents. *Hispanic Journal of the Behavioral Sciences, 16,* 28-42.

Ramos-McKay, J. M., Comas-Díaz, L., & Rivera, L. A. (1988). Puerto Ricans. In L. Comas-Díaz & E. E. H. Griffith (Eds.), *Clinical guidelines in cross-cultural mental health* (pp. 204-232). New York: John Wiley.

Reyhner, J., & Eder, J. (1988). A history of Indian education. In J. Reyhner (Ed.), *Teaching American Indian students* (2nd ed.) (pp. 33-58). Norman: University of Oklahoma Press.

Richardson, E. H. (1981). Cultural and historical perspectives in counseling American Indians. In D. W. Sue (Ed.), *Counseling the culturally different: Theory and practice* (pp. 216-255). New York: John Wiley.

Robins, L. N., Helzer, J. E., Weissman, M. W., Orvaschel, H., Gruenberg, E., Burke, J. D., & Regier, D. A. (1984). Lifetime prevalence of specific psychiatric disorders in three sites. *Archives of General Psychiatry, 41,* 949-958.

Robins, L. N., & Regier, D. A. (1991). *Psychiatric disorders in America: The epidemiologic catchment area study.* New York: Free Press.

Rogler, L. H. (1993). Culture in psychiatric diagnosis: An issue of scientific accuracy. *Psychiatry, 56,* 324-327.

Root, M., Ho, C., & Sue, S. (1986). Issues in the training of counselors for Asian Americans. In H. P. Lefley & P. B. Pedersen (Eds.), *Cross-cultural training for mental health professionals* (pp. 199-209). Springfield, IL: Charles C Thomas.

Rubel, A. J., O'Nell, C. W., & Collado-Ardon, R. (1984). *Susto: A folk illness.* Berkeley: University of California Press.

Ruiz, R. A. (1981). Cultural and historical perspectives in counseling Hispanics. In D. W. Sue (Ed.), *Counseling the culturally different: Theory and practice* (pp. 186-215). New York: John Wiley.

Ruiz, R. A., & Padilla, A. M. (1977). Counseling Latinos. *Personnel and Guidance Journal, 55,* 401-408.

Russell, D. M. (1988). Language and psychotherapy: The influence of nonstandard English in clinical practice. In L. Comas-Díaz & E. E. H. Griffith (Eds.), *Clinical guidelines in cross-cultural mental health* (pp. 33-68). New York: John Wiley.

Russo, N. F., Olmedo, E. L., Stapp, J., & Fulcher, R. (1981). Women and minorities in psychology. *American Psychologist, 36,* 1315-1363.

Sandoval, M. C., & De La Roza, M. C. (1986). A cultural perspective for serving Hispanic clients. In H. P. Lefley & P. B. Pedersen (Eds.), *Cross-cultural training for mental health professionals* (pp. 151-181). Springfield, IL: Charles C Thomas.

Seijo, R., Gomez, H., & Freidenberg, J. (1991). Language as a communication barrier in medical care for Hispanic patients. *Hispanic Journal of Behavioral Sciences, 13,* 363-376.

Simons, R. C., & Hughes, C. C. (1993). Cultural-bound syndromes. In A. C. Gaw (Ed.), *Culture, ethnicity, and mental illness* (pp. 75-93). Washington, DC: American Psychiatric Press.

Smith, E. J. (1981). Cultural and historical perspectives in counseling blacks. In D. W. (Ed.), *Counseling the culturally different: Theory and practice* (pp. 141-185). New York: John Wiley.

Smith, T. W. (1992). Changing racial labels: From "colored" to "negro" to "black" to "African American." *Public Opinion Quarterly, 56,* 496-544.

Smither, R., & Rodriguez-Giegling, M. (1982). Personality, demographics, and acculturation of Vietnamese and Nicaraguan refugees to the United States. *International Journal of Psychology, 17,* 19-25.

Soto, E. (1983). Sex-role traditionalism and assertiveness in Puerto Rican women living in the United States. *Journal of Community Psychology, 11,* 346-354.

Spitzer, R. L., & Endicott, J. (1978). *The schedule for affective disorders and schizophrenia* (3rd ed.). New York: New York State Psychiatric Institute.

Sue, D. W., & Sue, D. (1987). Asian-Americans and Pacific Islanders. In P. Pedersen (Ed.), *Handbook of cross-cultural counseling and therapy* (pp. 141-146). Westport, CT: Greenwood Press.

Sue, D. W., & Sue, D. (1990). *Counseling the culturally different: Theory and practice* (2nd ed.). New York: John Wiley.

Sue, S. (1988). Psychotherapy services for ethnic minorities: Two decades of research findings. *American Psychologist, 43,* 301-308.

Sue, S., Fujino, D. C., Hu, L., Takeuchi, D. T., & Zane, N. W. S. (1991). Community mental health services for ethnic minority groups: A test of the cultural responsiveness hypothesis. *Journal of Consulting and Clinical Psychology, 59,* 433-540.

Sue, S., & Zane, N. (1987). The role of culture and cultural techniques in psychotherapy. *American Psychologist, 42,* 37-45.

Suinn, R. M., Rickard-Figueroa, K., Lew, S., & Vigil, S. (1987). The Suinn-Lew Asian Self-Identity Acculturation scale: An initial report. *Education and Psychological Measurement, 47,* 401-407.

Szapocznik, J., Scopetta, M. A., Arnalde, M., & Kurtines, W. (1978). Cuban value structure: Treatment implications. *Journal of Consulting and Clinical Psychology, 46,* 961-970.

Taylor, R. J., & Chatters, L. M. (1986). Church-based informal support among elderly blacks. *The Gerontologist, 26,* 637-642.

Tharp, R. G. (1991). Cultural diversity and treatment of children. *Journal of Consulting and Clinical Psychology, 59,* 799-812.

Thompson, J., Walker, R. D., & Silk-Walker, P. (1993). Psychiatric care of American Indians and Alaska Natives. In A. C. Gaw (Ed.), *Culture, ethnicity, and mental illness* (pp. 189-243). Washington, DC: American Psychiatric Press.

Trimble, J. E., & Fleming, C. M. (1989). Providing counseling services for Native American Indians: Client, counselor, and community characteristics. In P. B. Pedersen, J. G. Dragnuns, W. J. Lonner, & J. E. Trimble (Eds.), *Counseling across cultures* (3rd ed.) (pp. 177-204). Honolulu: University of Hawaii Press.

Tsui, A. M. Psychotherapeutic consideration in sexual counseling for Asian immigrants. *Psychotherapy, 22,* 357-362.

U.S. Bureau of the Census (1983). *Statistical abstract of the United States.* Washington, DC: Government Printing Office.

U.S. Bureau of the Census (1992). *Statistical abstract of the United States.* Washington, DC: Government Printing Office.

U.S. Department of Health and Human Services (1991). *Health status of minorities and low-income groups: Third edition.* Washington, DC: Health Resources and Services Administration, U.S. Department of Health and Human Services.

Walker, R. D., & LaDue, R. (1986). An integrative approach to American Indian mental health. In C. B. Wilkinson (Ed.), *Ethnic psychiatry* (pp. 143-199). New York: Plenum.

Westermeyer, J. J. (1993). Cross-cultural psychiatric assessment. In A. C. Gaw (Ed.), *Culture, ethnicity, and mental illness* (pp. 125-144). Washington, DC: American Psychiatric Press.

Wilkinson, C. B. (1986). Introduction. In C. B. Wilkinson (Ed.), *Ethnic psychiatry* (pp. 1-11). New York: Plenum.

Wilkinson, C. B., & Spurlock, J. (1986). The mental health of black Americans: Psychiatric diagnosis and treatment. In C. B. Wilkinson (Ed.), *Ethnic psychiatry* (pp. 13-59). New York: Plenum.

Wilkinson, D. (1993). Family ethnicity in America. In H. P. McAdoo (Ed.), *Family ethnicity: Strength in diversity* (pp. 15-59). Newbury Park, CA: Sage.

Wise, F., & Miller, N. B. (1983). The mental health of American Indian children. In G. J. Powell, J. Yamamoto, A. Romero, & A. Morales (Eds.), *The psychosocial development of minority group children* (pp. 344-361). New York: Brunner/Mazel.

Wolpe, J., & Lang, P. J. (1964). A fear survey schedule for use in behavior therapy. *Behaviour Research and Therapy, 2,* 27-30.

Wong-Rieger, D., & Quintana, D. (1987). Comparative acculturation of Southeast Asians and Hispanic immigrants and sojourners. *Journal of Cross-Cultural Psychology, 18,* 145-162.

Yamamoto, J. (1986). Therapy for Asian Americans and Pacific Islanders. In C. B. Wilkinson (Ed.), *Ethnic psychiatry* (pp. 89-141). New York: Plenum.

Yamamoto, J., Silva, J. A., Justice, L. R., Chang, C. Y., & Leong, G. B. (1993). Cross-cultural psychotherapy. In A. C. Gaw (Ed.), *Culture, ethnicity, and mental illness* (pp. 101-124). Washington, DC: American Psychiatric Press.

Index

Acculturation:
    African Americans and, 26-27, 100
    American Indians and, 8
    Asians and, 69, 70
    assessment of, 120
    defined, 8
    ethnicity and, 4
    external, 8
    Hispanics and, 8, 44, 48, 50, 51, 100
    internal, 8
    interpretation of data and, 99
    interview process and, 99
    levels of, 9-10
    psychiatric epidemiology and, 99
Acculturation Balance Scale, 101
Acculturation Questionnaire, 101
Acculturation Rating Scale for Mexican
    Americans, 100, 101
African Americans:
    affiliation and, 21, 27-28
    Black English and, 23-24, 98
    cultural paranoia and, 22-23, 25
    depression and, 29
    discussion of racial differences and,
        24-26
    empowerment and, 33-35

    familism and, 20
    family secrets and, 30-31, 93
    grandmother and, 28-29
    income and, 19
    internal acculturation and, 27
    medication and, 22
    poverty and, 19
    racial labels and, 20
    religious beliefs and, 21-22
    role flexibility and, 21, 32
    schizophrenia and, 29-30
    standard American English and, 23
    street talk and, 23-24
    strengths of, 32
    substance abuse and, 29-30
    voodoo priests and, 22
American Indians:
    alcoholism and, 84, 87, 88
    assimilation period and, 77-78
    boarding schools and, 77, 86
    collectivism and, 81, 82
    confidentiality and, 83-84
    definition of "Indian" and, 74
    depression and, 84
    discrimination of, 76, 77
    epidemics and, 76-77, 86

European diseases and, 76, 77
eye contact and, 81
familism and, 79-80
foster care and, 89
handshake and, 81
income and, 74
individualism and, 81-82
manifest destiny period and, 76-77
medicine men and, 76, 80, 83, 85, 87,
    88, 116
medicine women, 80, 83, 85, 87, 88, 116
nonverbal communication and, 81
precontact period and, 75-76
racism and, 76, 77
relocation and, 78
reservations and, 74, 77, 86, 103
role of Christianity and, 77
rules and, 79-80
self-determination period and, 78-79
sharing and, 80
survival pact and, 76-77, 86
taking notes and, 83
termination and, 78
time and, 80, 94
treatment of children and, 89
voting privileges and, 78
Asians:
conversational distance and, 59
community services and, 62
discrimination and, 56
divorce and, 70, 71
duration of interview with, 64
duration of therapy and, 67
familism and, 56-57
formalism and, 59
forms of communication and, 558-559
hospitalization and, 61-62, 94
income and, 55-56
personalism and, 67, 94
prejudice and, 56
racism and, 56
role flexibility and, 57
role of children and, 57
role of women and, 57
saving face and, 70
shame and, 57, 60, 61, 66-67, 70, 92,
    94, 111
somatization and, 60-61
suicidal behavior and, 61
suppression of problems and, 57-58
talking therapy and, 71

Attrition:
defined, 91
strategies to prevent, 91
with African American clients, 31, 93
with American Indian clients, 94
with Asian clients, 94
with Hispanic clients, 49, 93

Beck Depression Inventory, 120
Behavioral Acculturation Scale, 100, 101
Behavioral Approaches:
ethnicity and, 52
race and, 52
survival pact and, 86
with American Indian clients, 86
with Asian clients, 68
with Hispanic clients, 51-52
Bias:
assessment and, 105, 106
cross-cultural testing and, 106
culture-free tests and, 105
degree of, 119-120
racism and, 106, 110-111
reporting data and, 100
sample and, 102, 103, 104
self-evaluation of, 107-110
Brief Acculturation Scale, 11, 51

California Psychological Inventory, 120
Center for Epidemiologic Studies Depres-
    sion Scale, 121
Child Behavior Checklist, 113
Children's Acculturation Scale, 101
Code switching:
bilingual clients and, 98
defined, 98
Conceptual equivalence:
culture-free tests and, 105-106
defined, 106
Content equivalence:
culture-free tests and, 105-106
defined, 105
Credibility defined, 8
Criterion equivalence:
culture-free tests and, 105-106
defined, 105
Cross-cultural validity defined, 13
Cuban Behavioral Identity Questionnaire,
    101

Cuento Therapy, Hispanics and, 54
Cultural-bound syndromes. *See* Cultural-
related syndromes
Cultural compatibility hypothesis defined, 6
Cultural competence defined, 7
Cultural equivalence:
culture-free tests and, 105-106
defined, 105
Cultural Fair Intelligence Test, 121
Cultural Life Style Inventory, 101
Cultural match, 6
Cultural mismatch, 6, 7
Cultural-related syndromes:
assessment and, 106, 112-115
examples of, 112
mental disorders and, 112
psychiatric disorders and, 115
reimbursement practices and, 114
unethical behaviors and, 114
unfair discriminatory practices and, 114
Cultural sensitivity defined, 7
Cultural-specific disorders. *See* Cultural-
related syndromes
Cultural validity:
acculturation and, 99-100
code switching and, 98
defined, 97
folk beliefs and, 99
language and, 97-98
Curandero(a), bruja(o) versus, 48

Developmental Inventory of Black Con-
sciousness, 99, 101
Diagnostic and Statistical Manual of
Mental Disorders:
culture-related syndromes and, 114
racism and, 110
Diversity. *See* Multicultural
Doña defined, 46
Don defined, 46
Draw-A-Person Test, 121

Emit perspective:
behavioral observation and, 122
defined, 122
life history and, 122
Enfermedad mental, estar loco versus, 44
Ethnic Identity Questionnaire, 101
Ethnicity defined, 4

Ethnic match, minimizing biases and, 112
Extended family:
African Americans and, 14, 15, 28-29,
32, 34
American Indians and, 15, 79
Asians and, 14, 56
defined, 14-15
foster homes and, 16
Hispanics and, 15, 41
versus family tree, 15
Eysenck Personality Questionnaire, 121

Family therapy:
familism and, 50
with African American clients, 34-35
with American Indian clients, 87
with Asian clients, 57, 68-70
with Hispanic clients, 50
Fear Survey Schedule, 120
Fetal alcohol syndrome, American Indians
and, 84
Folk beliefs:
diagnosis and, 99
effects on incidence, 99
effects on prevalence, 99

Giving, defined, 8
Group Therapy:
with American Indian clients, 88
with Asian clients, 71
with Hispanic clients, 50

Hispanics:
acculturation and, 44-46
assertive behavior and, 52
curandero(a) and, 39, 47-48, 115
dating and, 45, 50, 51
defined, 38
espiritista and, 39, 47, 115
external acculturation and, 44
familismo and, 40-41, 52
fatalismo and, 42-43
folk beliefs and, 39
formalismo and, 46-47, 49, 93
income, 38
individualismo and, 42
internal acculturation and, 44
level of acculturation and, 44-45

machismo and, 39, 45, 51, 52, 54, 93
madrina and, 41
mal de ojo and, 39, 49, 93, 99
marianismo and, 40, 45, 52, 93
padrino and, 41
personalismo and, 41-42, 46-47, 49-50,
    93
religion and, 39
respeto and, 39, 40, 52
role flexibility and, 41
skin color and, 43-44
susto and, 49
Holtzman Inkblot Technique, 121

Incidence, defined, 95
Indian Child Welfare Act:
    American Indian children and, 79
    elements of, 79
    foster care and, 79
Indian Health Care Improvement Act, 78
Indian Health Service, 103
Indian Religious Freedom Act, 78
Indian Reorganization Act, 78
Indian Self-Determination Act, 78
Insight-Oriented Therapy, Hispanics and,
    54

Kaufman Assessment Battery for Children,
    121

Language:
    Black English and, 98
    code switching and, 98
    psychopathology and, 97-98
    standard American English and, 97
Leiter International Performance Scale,
    121

Medication:
    with African Americans clients, 93
    with American Indian clients, 83, 88
    with Asians clients, 64, 67-68
    with Hispanic clients, 48-49, 53-54, 93
Mental status examination:
    bias and, 106, 116-119
    components of, 117-118

Minnesota Multiphasic Personality
        Inventory:
    acculturation and, 99
    African Americans and, 116
    cultural-related syndromes and, 113
    folk beliefs and, 99
    Hispanics and, 116, 122
Minority defined, 1-3
Multicultural Acculturation Scale, 101
Multicultural Experience Inventory, 101
Multicultural group defined, 3
Music therapy, Hispanics and, 54

Organizations for American Indians, 75,
    89-90

Paraprofessionals, minimizing bias and,
    116
Plains culture, 100
Plains Indians. See Plains culture
Prevalence defined, 95
Progressive matrices, 121
Psychodynamic model, American Indian
    clients and, 88
Psychotherapy, Asian clients and, 63

Race:
    defined, 4
    diagnosis and, 110-111
Racial Identity Attitude Scale, 99, 101
Racial match:
    defined, 6
    minimizing bias and, 112
Racism:
    defined, 110
    overdiagnosing and, 110
    underdiagnosing and, 110
Rational-Emotive Therapy, Hispanics and,
    54
Rosebud Personal Opinion Survey, 100,
    101

Schedule for Affective Disorders and
    Schizophrenia, 121
Self-Evaluation of Biases and Prejudice
    Scale, 108-109

Semantic equivalence:
   culture-free tests and, 105-106
   defined, 105
Serial 7s Test, mental status and, 117
Social-skills training:
   with African American clients, 33-34
   with American Indian clients, 86
   with Hispanic clients, 52
   with southeast Asian refugees and, 72
Socio-cultural gap:
   assessment and, 112
   diagnosis and, 112
Socioeconomic variables:
   biases and, 111
   diagnosis and, 111
Southeast Asian refugees:
   brain syndrome and, 65
   extended family and, 71
   family therapy and, 71
   social services and, 71
   stress reduction and, 66
   suicide attempt and, 65
   traumatic events and, 65-72
Suinn-Lew Asian Self-Identity Accultura-
      tion Scale, 101
Systematic desensitization, Hispanics
      clients and, 52

System of Multicultural Pluralistic
      Assessment, 121

Technical equivalence:
   culture-free tests and, 105-106
   defined, 105
Tell-Me-A-Story Test, 120, 121
Therapeutic relationship, development of,
      5-8
Therapist defined across multicultural
      groups, 18
Translators, guidelines when using,
      12-13

Usted:
   formalism and, 46
   tu versus, 46

Wechsler Adult Intelligence Scale, 122,
      123

Zung Depression Scale, 113

About the Author

Freddy A. Paniagua (Ph.D., University of Kansas, Postdoctoral Training at The Johns Hopkins University School of Medicine) is Associate Professor in the Department of Psychiatry and Behavioral Sciences, University of Texas Medical Branch at Galveston, where he teaches cross-cultural mental health seminars with emphasis on the assessment and treatment of African American, Hispanic, Asian, and American Indian clients. He has received funding since 1989 from the National Institute of Mental Health to provide postdoctoral and postmaster training to mental health professionals representing different multicultural groups, with emphasis on the assessment and treatment of emotionally disturbed clients. He has published more than 30 scientific articles, including basic and applied research and theoretical contributions.